I0616321

Mourning into Morning: 31 Affirmations for Those Who Are Grieving

Valora Richardson, PhD

DESTINED INNOVATIONS

Copyright © 2025 by Destined Innovations, LLC

Scripture quotations marked (NIV) are taken from the Holy Bible, New International Version®, NIV®. Copyright © 1973, 1978, 1984, 2011 by Biblica, Inc.™ Used by permission of Zondervan. All rights reserved worldwide. www.zondervan.comThe "NIV" and "New International Version" are trademarks registered in the United States Patent and Trademark Office by Biblica, Inc.™

Scripture quotations marked (NLT) are taken from the Holy Bible, New Living Translation, copyright © 1996, 2004, 2015 by Tyndale House Foundation. Used by permission of Tyndale House Publishers, Carol Stream, Illinois 60188.

This document was drafted with partial assistance from artificial intelligence.

All rights reserved.

In Memoriam

Peter Daniel Cunningham-Richardson

February 26, 1969 - May 22.2022

Blessed be the God and Father of our Lord Jesus Christ, the Father of mercies and God of all comfort, who comforts us in all our affliction, so that we may be able to comfort those who are in any affliction, with the comfort with which we ourselves are comforted by God.

2 Corinthians 1:4 ESV

Dedication

This book is dedicated to my daughters, Anaia and Alaina. Your strength and resilience in our time of loss has been my inspiration. I am so proud of you and look forward to what God will do in our next chapter.

Table of Contents

Preface

When we lose someone we love, the world keeps moving, often faster than we can manage. In still moments, we are left with our thoughts, tears, and longing.

Morning into Mourning: 31 Affirmations and Prayers for Those Who Are Grieving emerged from my own loss and the understanding that healing has no one-size-fits-all approach. For those navigating this path, some days begin with hope, while others feel heavy with sorrow. I hope this book serves as a gentle companion—a guide to help you take each day one step at a time.

Scripture assures us that God is close to the brokenhearted (Psalm 34:18). Each affirmation and prayer in this book is rooted in God's Word, offering comfort whether you face fresh pain, moments of peace, or need a reminder that you are not alone. These reflections don't rush your healing but provide solace, strength, and the assurance of God's love as you journey from mourning to morning.

Jesus said, "Blessed are those who mourn, for they will be comforted" (Matthew 5:4). Grief is not something to overcome; it is a testament to the love you shared and the impact of the one you've lost.

As you explore these pages, may you find comfort knowing you are not alone. Whether read in the quiet of the morning, moments of stillness, or before bed, may these words bring you peace and connection—to yourself, your loved one, and the divine presence that sustains us all. Let Scripture and prayer guide you, reminding you of the eternal hope we have in Christ.

With love and compassion,
Valora

Introduction

Grieving is often described as a rollercoaster, full of highs and lows that come without warning. It's a process that requires patience, grace, and the willingness to allow God to meet us in our brokenness. This book is not just a collection of affirmations and prayers but a hands-on tool to help you process your grief, day by day, with the support of Scripture and guided reflection.

Each day of Morning into Mourning is designed to be a sacred space for you to connect with your emotions, your faith, and your healing. The daily structure includes several elements to support you in this journey:

Affirmation and Scripture Passage: Begin each day with an uplifting affirmation and a carefully chosen Bible verse. These words will serve as a reminder of God's presence and promises, even in the midst of pain.

Reflection Question: A question prompts you to think deeply about the affirmation and Scripture. This is your opportunity to explore what these truths mean to you personally and how they resonate with your journey.

Daily Self-Care Plan: Grief can be physically, emotionally, and spiritually draining. Take a moment to write down one way you will care for yourself that day. It could be something as simple as taking a walk, calling a friend, or spending time in prayer.

Something to Look Forward To: Hope can feel distant during grief, but looking forward to even the smallest joys can make a difference. Write about something—big or small—that brings you a glimmer of anticipation.

Gratitude Journal: On the following page, you will find space to list what you are grateful for. Gratitude doesn't negate grief, but it can offer moments of light in the darkness.

Mood Tracker: Use the mood tracker to record how you are feeling that day. This simple exercise helps you become more aware of your emotions and notice patterns over time.

Reflection on Improvement: There is also space to write about what could make you feel better. This isn't about fixing your grief but identifying small, actionable steps that could help ease the burden.

Requests: Finally, write down your prayer requests. These may include prayers for comfort, strength, or guidance. By putting your requests into words, you invite God to work in those areas of your life.

This book is not about rushing through grief or finding a quick fix. It's about honoring your emotions, leaning on God's Word, and creating space for healing. Each day, give yourself grace. You are not alone on this journey, and my prayer is that these pages will provide you with the support, encouragement, and peace you need.

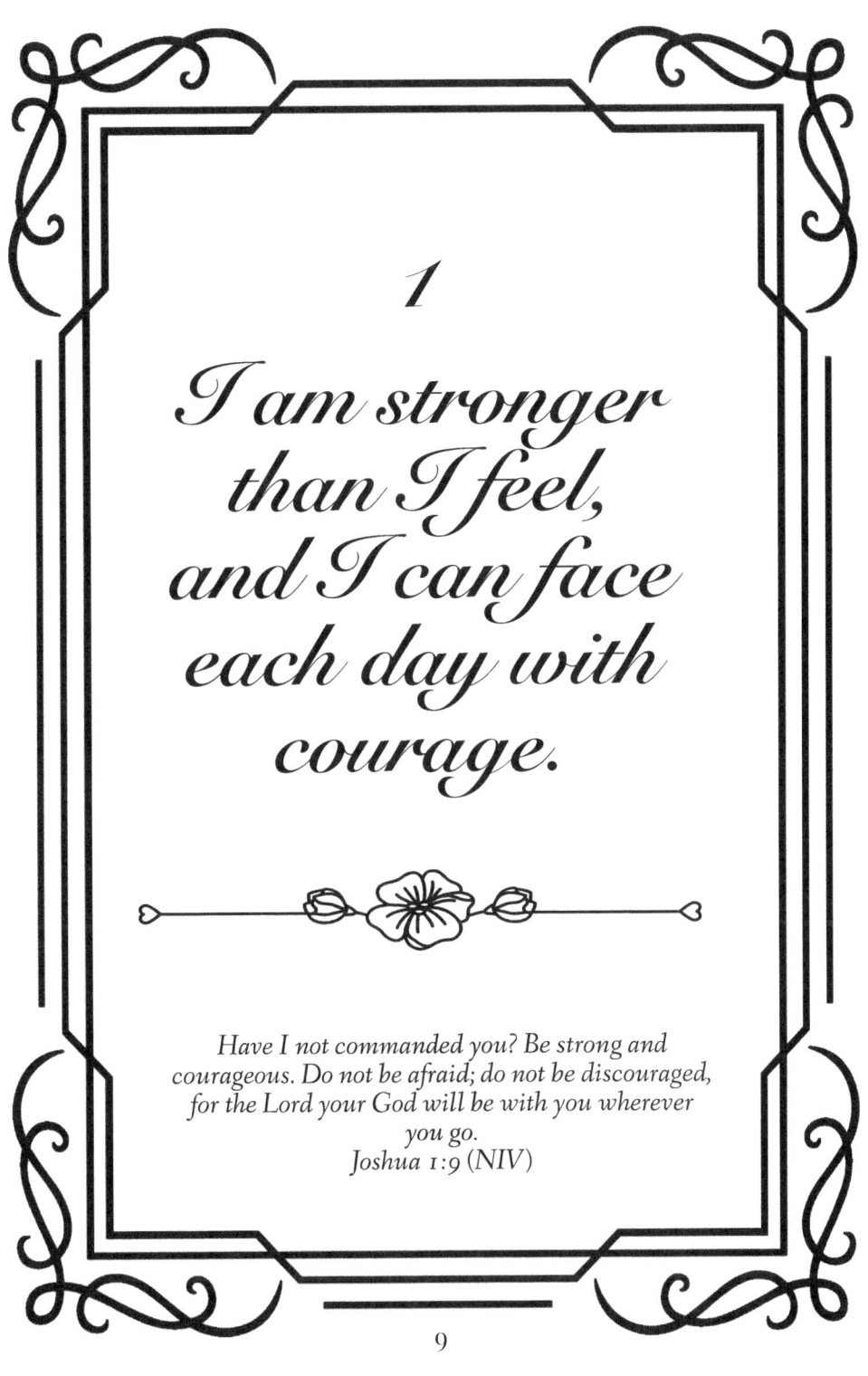

1

I am stronger than I feel, and I can face each day with courage.

Have I not commanded you? Be strong and
courageous. Do not be afraid; do not be discouraged,
for the Lord your God will be with you wherever
you go.
Joshua 1:9 (NIV)

Reflection

Grief can feel like uncharted territory—overwhelming, uncertain, and exhausting. Joshua 1:9 assures us that we are not meant to walk this path alone. God's presence is our anchor, offering strength when ours feels depleted and courage when fear takes hold.

This call to be strong is not about suppressing pain but about trusting that God walks with us, even in our brokenness. It takes courage to face each day, to grieve fully, and to believe in healing. Yet, God's promise remains: He goes before us, beside us, and carries us through.

On the hardest days, when discouragement sets in, He provides more than a command—He provides Himself. His presence renews our strength, His peace calms our fear, and His love fills the emptiness. We do not have to rely on our own strength; we are held by the One who never leaves us. With Him, we can keep moving forward, step by step, toward hope and healing.

A Prayer for Strength and Courage

Dear Lord,

Thank You for being my refuge and source of strength. In moments when I feel weak and overwhelmed, remind me of the courage You have placed within me. Help me to trust in Your power to sustain me and guide me through every challenge I face.

Give me the faith to take each day one step at a time, knowing that You are always by my side. When my spirit feels weary, renew my strength, and when my heart feels heavy, lift my burdens.

Lord, I declare that with Your help, I am stronger than I feel. Fill me with peace and boldness to face the unknown, confident in Your promises and love. Thank You for walking this journey with me and for the courage You provide each day.

In Jesus' name, I pray,

Amen

Where have you seen evidence of your strength and courage?

_____

_____

_____

_____

_____

_____

_____

_____

_____

_____

_____

_____

Today I feel

I will feel better tomorrow when I…

_____

_____

_____

_____

_____

_____

I am grateful for...

_____
_____
_____
_____
_____
_____
_____
_____
_____
_____
_____
_____

Things to pray about...

_____
_____
_____
_____
_____
_____
_____

2

I honor my loved one by continuing to live with purpose and grace.

Many are the plans in a person's heart, but it is the Lord's purpose that prevails.
Proverbs 19:21 (NIV)

Reflection

Loss often disrupts our carefully laid plans, leaving us feeling vulnerable or disoriented. In these moments, This verse invites us to surrender our need for control and trust in God's overarching plan. It reassures us that, even when life seems chaotic or unfair, God is weaving a story of redemption, meaning, and grace.

Seeking God's purpose does not mean abandoning our dreams or aspirations but aligning them with His will. Through prayer, scripture, and reflection, we can discern His guidance, allowing His plans to take precedence over our own. This alignment often brings peace and clarity, even in the face of uncertainty.

God's purposes are always good and perfect. While we may not always understand why certain things happen, we can trust that His plans are designed to lead us into a life of fulfillment, spiritual growth, and deeper connection with Him.

We are encouraged to hold our plans loosely and embrace faith, knowing that God's purpose will not only prevail but will also bring us closer to a life infused with grace, meaning, and hope—even in the face of pain or loss.

A Prayer for Purpose and Grace

Dear Lord,

Thank You for the time I shared with my loved one and for the memories that will always live in my heart. As I move forward, I ask for Your guidance to live a life filled with purpose and grace. Help me to honor their legacy by embracing the gifts You have given me and sharing them with the world.

Strengthen me to find joy and meaning in each day, even as I carry the weight of my loss. Let my actions reflect the love and lessons I hold dear, and may they be a testament to the beauty of their life.

Grant me the courage to face challenges with faith, the wisdom to seek Your will, and the peace to trust in Your plan for my future. With Your help, I will walk this path with grace, honoring both my loved one and Your eternal love.

In Jesus' name, I pray,
Amen.

How can you honor your loved one through purposeful and graceful living?

_____
_____
_____
_____
_____
_____
_____
_____
_____
_____
_____
_____
_____

Today I feel

I will feel better tomorrow when I...

_____
_____
_____
_____
_____

I am grateful for...

_____
_____
_____
_____
_____
_____
_____
_____
_____
_____
_____
_____

Things to pray about...

_____
_____
_____
_____
_____
_____
_____
_____

3

It's okay to grieve and heal at my own pace.

*There is a time for everything, and a season for
every activity under the heavens... a time to weep
and a time to laugh, a time to mourn
and a time to dance.*
Ecclesiastes 3:1, 4 (NIV)

Reflection

Ecclesiastes 3:1, 4 affirms that grief is not a detour in life but a necessary season within its rhythm. Mourning has its place, just as joy does. It is not meant to be rushed or dismissed but honored as a sacred space for healing.

This passage embraces the full spectrum of human emotion. Grief and joy are not opposites; they coexist. Some days, sorrow may feel overwhelming, yet glimpses of peace or laughter will begin to break through. Healing is not about forgetting but about allowing both weeping and joy to shape our journey.

Like the changing seasons, grief unfolds in its own time. There is no right pace—only the path uniquely meant for us. And while mourning is real, so is the promise of renewal. In time, sorrow will give way to joy, and the weight of loss will make space for moments of light once more.

By allowing ourselves to grieve, we honor both our loss and the love that came before it. Trusting God's timing, we can move forward with grace, knowing that in His perfect season, joy will return.

A Prayer for Grace in Grieving

Dear Lord,

I thank you for Your endless patience and compassion. In this season of grief, I ask for Your reassurance that it's okay to heal at my own pace. Help me to release the pressure to move forward too quickly and instead embrace each step of this journey with gentleness and grace.

Remind me, Lord, that You see my pain and understand my heart even when words fail me. Guide me to be kind to myself, allowing space for both sorrow and hope to coexist. Surround me with Your peace, and help me to trust that You are bringing healing in Your perfect timing.

Thank You for walking beside me through this process, comforting me when I need it and strengthening me when I feel weak. I place my grief in Your hands, knowing that Your love will lead me toward wholeness.

In Jesus' name, I pray,
Amen.

What does grieving at your own pace look like for you, and how can you embrace it without judgment?

_____

_____

_____

_____

_____

_____

_____

_____

_____

_____

_____

_____

_____

Today I feel

I will feel better tomorrow when I…

_____

_____

_____

_____

_____

_____

I am grateful for…

_____
_____
_____
_____
_____
_____
_____
_____
_____
_____
_____

Things to pray about…

_____
_____
_____
_____
_____
_____
_____

4

Each day, I grow stronger and more resilient.

"But those who hope in the Lord will renew their strength. They will soar on wings like eagles; they will run and not grow weary, they will walk and not be faint."
Isaiah 40:31

Reflection

Grief can feel like an unshakable weight, draining our strength and making each day a struggle. Isaiah 40:31 offers a lifeline—not by dismissing our sorrow, but by inviting us to place our hope in the Lord, who sustains us through every tear and every heartache.

Eagles don't escape the wind; they rise on it. In the same way, God doesn't always remove our grief, but He lifts us through it. His strength carries us when ours fails, helping us find moments of peace and meaning even in the pain.

Some days, grief feels like a race we're too weary to finish; other days, simply standing feels impossible. Yet, this verse promises that God will give us exactly what we need— renewed strength for every step, endurance for the journey, and the courage to keep moving forward.

Hope in the Lord is more than a feeling; it is a source of unshakable strength. He walks with us, lifts us, and assures us that grief will not last forever. Through Him, we can keep walking, keep healing, and one day, soar again.

A Prayer for Strength and Resilience

Dear Lord,

Thank You for the strength You provide me each day, even when I don't always feel it. As I journey through this season, I trust that You are shaping me into someone stronger and more resilient. Help me to see the small victories and progress I make, knowing that each step forward is a testament to Your faithfulness in my life.

Lord, continue to renew my mind and spirit, filling me with courage and perseverance. When challenges arise, remind me that with You, I can overcome them. Teach me to lean on Your promises and to find hope in Your unchanging love.

I am grateful for the resilience You are building in me. May it not only carry me through my trials but also allow me to be a source of encouragement and light to others.

In Jesus' name, I pray,

Amen.

In what ways have you grown stronger and more resilient over time, and how can you celebrate that growth?

_____
_____
_____
_____
_____
_____
_____
_____
_____
_____
_____
_____
_____

Today I feel

I will feel better tomorrow when I…

_____
_____
_____
_____
_____
_____

I am grateful for…

_____
_____
_____
_____
_____
_____
_____
_____
_____
_____
_____

Things to pray about…

_____
_____
_____
_____
_____
_____
_____
_____

5

I carry forward the best of what we shared.

Finally, brothers and sisters, whatever is true, whatever is noble, whatever is right, whatever is pure, whatever is lovely, whatever is admirable—if anything is excellent or praiseworthy— think about such things.
Philippians 4:8 (NIV)

Reflection

Grief often overwhelms the heart and mind with sorrow, confusion, and sometimes despair. Philippians 4:8 provides a powerful framework for navigating grief, offering guidance on where to direct our thoughts during times of loss. It reminds us that even in our pain, we can choose to anchor ourselves in what is true, noble, and praiseworthy.

When grieving, reflecting on the truth—such as the love we shared with the one we've lost—grounds us in the reality that their life had meaning and impact. Focusing on what is noble and admirable can remind us of their virtues and the positive legacy they left behind. By dwelling on the pure and lovely memories, we honor their presence in our lives and find moments of comfort amidst the sorrow.

This doesn't mean ignoring or suppressing grief; rather, it's about allowing space for hope and gratitude alongside the pain. Thinking on what is excellent and praiseworthy can help us move forward with resilience, carrying forward the best of what they gave us—their love, wisdom, and joy—into our lives and relationships.

In this way, Philippians 4:8 becomes a guide for honoring the memory of those we've lost while finding light and strength to continue living meaningfully. It helps us reframe our grief as a reflection of love and reminds us to focus on the goodness we've experienced, even in the face of loss.

A Prayer for Carrying Forward Love and Lessons

Dear Lord,

Thank You for the love and experiences I shared with my loved one. Though they are no longer with me, I carry forward the best of what we shared—the love, lessons, and memories that continue to shape me.

Help me to honor their legacy in the way I live my life. May the kindness, joy, and wisdom we shared inspire my actions and guide my path. Teach me to hold onto these gifts with gratitude while stepping forward into the future You have prepared for me.

Thank You, Lord, for allowing their impact to live on in me and for walking with me as I embrace this next chapter.

In Jesus' name, I pray,

Amen.

What lessen did your loved one teach you that you carry with you?

_____
_____
_____
_____
_____
_____
_____
_____
_____
_____
_____
_____
_____

Today I feel

I will feel better tomorrow when I...

_____
_____
_____
_____
_____
_____

I am grateful for...

_____
_____
_____
_____
_____
_____
_____
_____
_____
_____
_____

Things to pray about...

_____
_____
_____
_____
_____
_____
_____

6

My heart expands to hold both grief and joy.

Weeping may stay for the night,
but rejoicing comes in the morning.
Psalm 30:5 (NIV)

Reflection

Joy is a promise from God—a gift that will return, bringing light after the darkness of mourning. Psalm 30:5 offers us comfort and hope, reminding us that grief, though heavy and overwhelming at times, is temporary and not without purpose.

This passage speaks to the resilience of the human spirit, created by God to endure sorrow while still being capable of experiencing joy. It encourages us to lean into the grieving process without fear, trusting that the pain we feel is not permanent. Just as night gives way to morning, our periods of sadness will eventually give way to moments of peace, hope, and rejoicing.

As we heal and grow, this verse reminds us that both grief and joy are integral to our journey. Grief teaches us to cherish what we've lost and deepens our capacity for compassion, while joy reminds us of God's unchanging faithfulness and His ability to restore our hearts. Together, these emotions shape us, allowing us to experience the fullness of life and the richness of God's grace. Through this promise, we are invited to hold on to hope, even in our darkest nights, knowing that morning will bring new mercies and renewed strength.

A Prayer for Embracing Grief and Joy

Dear Lord,

Thank You for creating my heart with the capacity to hold both grief and joy. Help me to embrace the fullness of my emotions, knowing that sorrow and happiness can coexist as part of my healing journey.

Teach me to honor my grief without fear and to welcome moments of joy as reminders of Your love and faithfulness. May my heart continue to expand with Your grace, allowing me to experience the depth of both emotions and the beauty of life.

Thank You, Lord, for walking with me through this journey and for filling my heart with hope, even in the midst of pain.

In Jesus' name, I pray,

Amen.

What brings you comfort in your grief?

_____
_____
_____
_____
_____
_____
_____
_____
_____
_____
_____

Today I feel

I will feel better tomorrow when I...

_____
_____
_____
_____
_____
_____

I am grateful for…

_____
_____
_____
_____
_____
_____
_____
_____
_____
_____
_____

Things to pray about…

_____
_____
_____
_____
_____
_____
_____

7

I am capable of creating a meaningful and joyful life again.

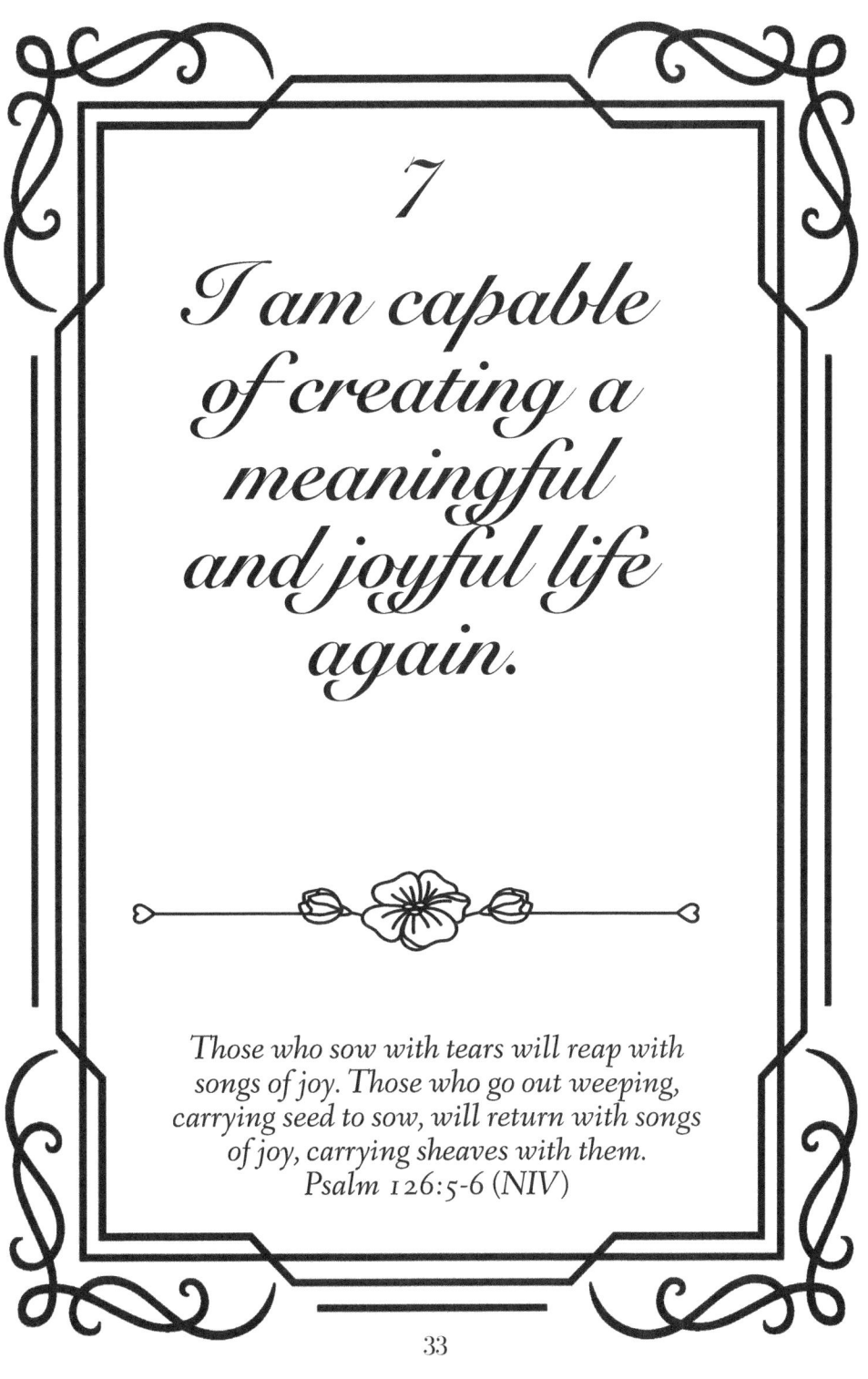

Those who sow with tears will reap with songs of joy. Those who go out weeping, carrying seed to sow, will return with songs of joy, carrying sheaves with them.
Psalm 126:5-6 (NIV)

Reflection

Psalm 126:5-6 offers a profound promise: sorrow is not the end of the story. Tears, though painful, are not wasted—they are seeds planted in faith, leading to a future of joy and renewal.

Sowing in tears acknowledges the weight of grief. Every step forward can feel exhausting, yet even in our brokenness, our prayers, perseverance, and small acts of trust hold meaning. God sees our sorrow and honors the courage it takes to keep moving, even when our hearts are heavy.

The promise of reaping with joy assures us that seasons of sorrow are temporary. Just as seeds grow in time, grief, when surrendered to God, transforms into renewed purpose and hope. This joy does not erase pain but redeems it, allowing us to live fully again while honoring the love we've lost.

Even in weeping, we are planting seeds—acts of kindness, steps toward healing, quiet moments of trust. God is working through our pain, bringing forth something beautiful. The tears we sow today will yield a harvest of grace, reminding us that with Him, sorrow will always give way to joy.

A Prayer for Renewal and Joy

Dear Lord,

Thank You for Your promise of renewal and hope. Even in the midst of loss and pain, I trust in Your power to restore my heart and guide me toward a life filled with meaning and joy. Help me to believe that I am capable, through Your strength, of building a beautiful and purposeful future.=

Grant me the courage to take steps forward, even when it feels uncertain. Open my eyes to new opportunities for growth, connection, and fulfillment. Remind me that the joy You offer is not dependent on circumstances but is rooted in Your unfailing love.

Lord, let my life reflect Your grace and goodness as I rebuild it. Teach me to walk in hope, to embrace each new day, and to trust that You are creating something beautiful from my pain.

In Jesus' name, I pray,
Amen.

How are you learning to live with your loss?

_____
_____
_____
_____
_____
_____
_____
_____
_____
_____
_____
_____
_____
_____

Today I feel

I will feel better tomorrow when I...

_____
_____
_____
_____
_____
_____
_____

I am grateful for...

_____
_____
_____
_____
_____
_____
_____
_____
_____
_____
_____
_____

Things to pray about...

_____
_____
_____
_____
_____
_____
_____
_____

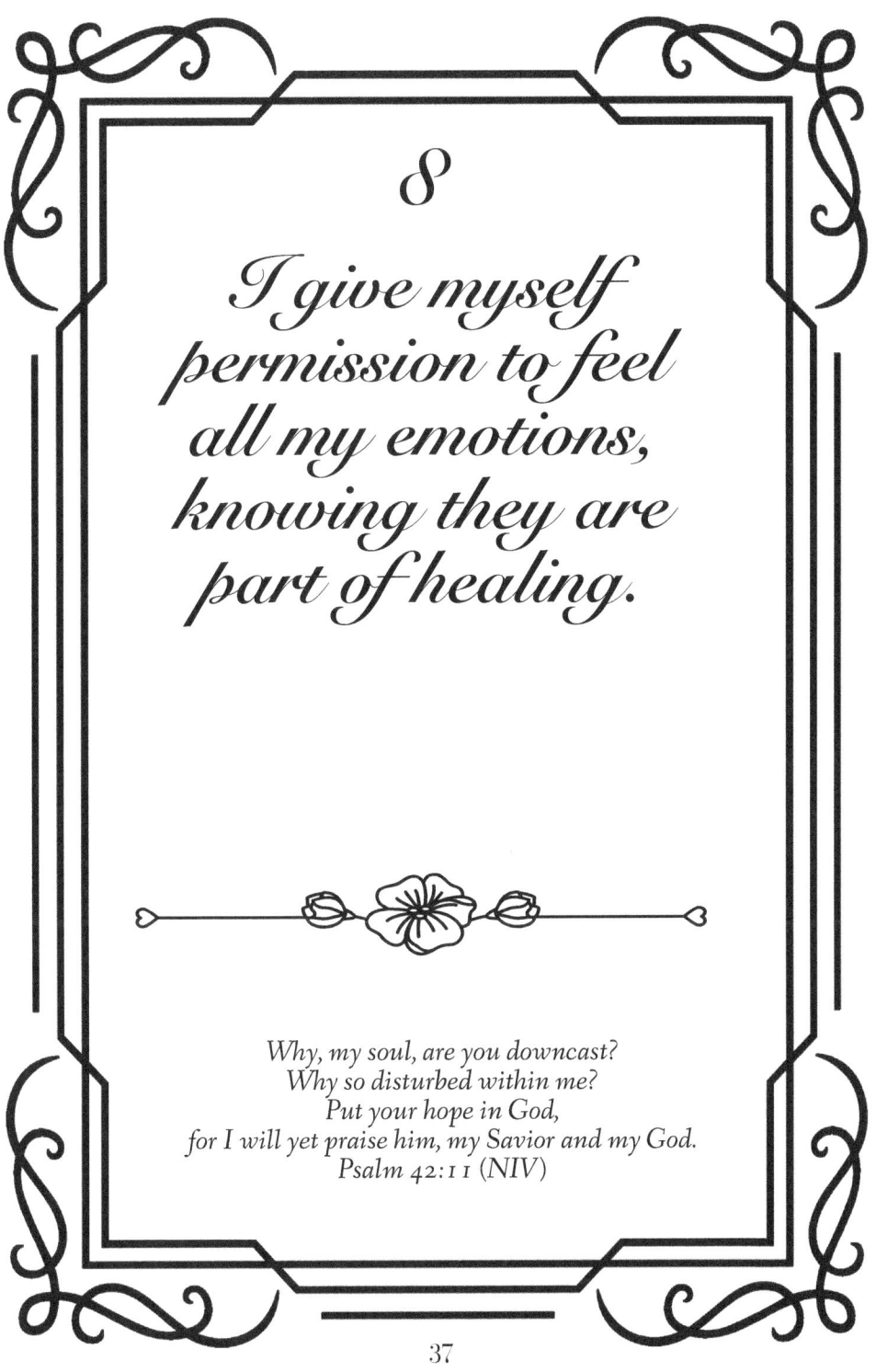

8

I give myself permission to feel all my emotions, knowing they are part of healing.

Why, my soul, are you downcast?
Why so disturbed within me?
Put your hope in God,
for I will yet praise him, my Savior and my God.
Psalm 42:11 (NIV)

Reflection

Psalm 42:11 captures the tension between deep sorrow and unwavering faith. The psalmist's raw honesty—"Why, my soul, are you downcast?"—acknowledges the weight of grief without shame. These words remind us that sadness, despair, and turmoil are natural parts of the human experience, not signs of weak faith.

Yet, the verse doesn't end in despair. "Put your hope in God, for I will yet praise Him" is a declaration that grief and hope can coexist. Pain is real, but it is not the final word. Trusting God in our lowest moments opens the door for His renewal, even when healing feels far away.

This verse invites us to be honest about our struggles while holding on to the certainty of God's faithfulness. Sorrow may linger, but hope remains—anchored in the promise that God will sustain, restore, and lead us to praise once again.

A Prayer for Emotional Healing

Dear Lord,

I am grateful that you have created me with the ability to feel deeply. I bring to You my full range of emotions—grief, sadness, anger, confusion, and even moments of peace and joy. I give myself permission to feel them all, trusting that they are part of the healing process You are leading me through.

Help me not to suppress or rush my feelings but to embrace them as an expression of my humanity and a step toward restoration. Grant me the wisdom to discern when to rest, when to release, and when to lean on others for support. Surround me with Your peace as I navigate this journey.

Thank You, Lord, for being patient with me and for walking beside me as I heal. Remind me that I am not alone and that every tear I shed matters to You. I trust in Your promise to bring beauty and wholeness from my brokenness.

In Jesus' name, I pray,

Amen.

What permissions are you giving yourself?

_____

_____

_____

_____

_____

_____

_____

_____

_____

_____

_____

_____

_____

Today I feel

I will feel better tomorrow when I...

_____

_____

_____

_____

_____

_____

I am grateful for…

_____
_____
_____
_____
_____
_____
_____
_____
_____
_____
_____

Things to pray about…

_____
_____
_____
_____
_____
_____
_____

9
Healing is a journey, and I honor every step I take.

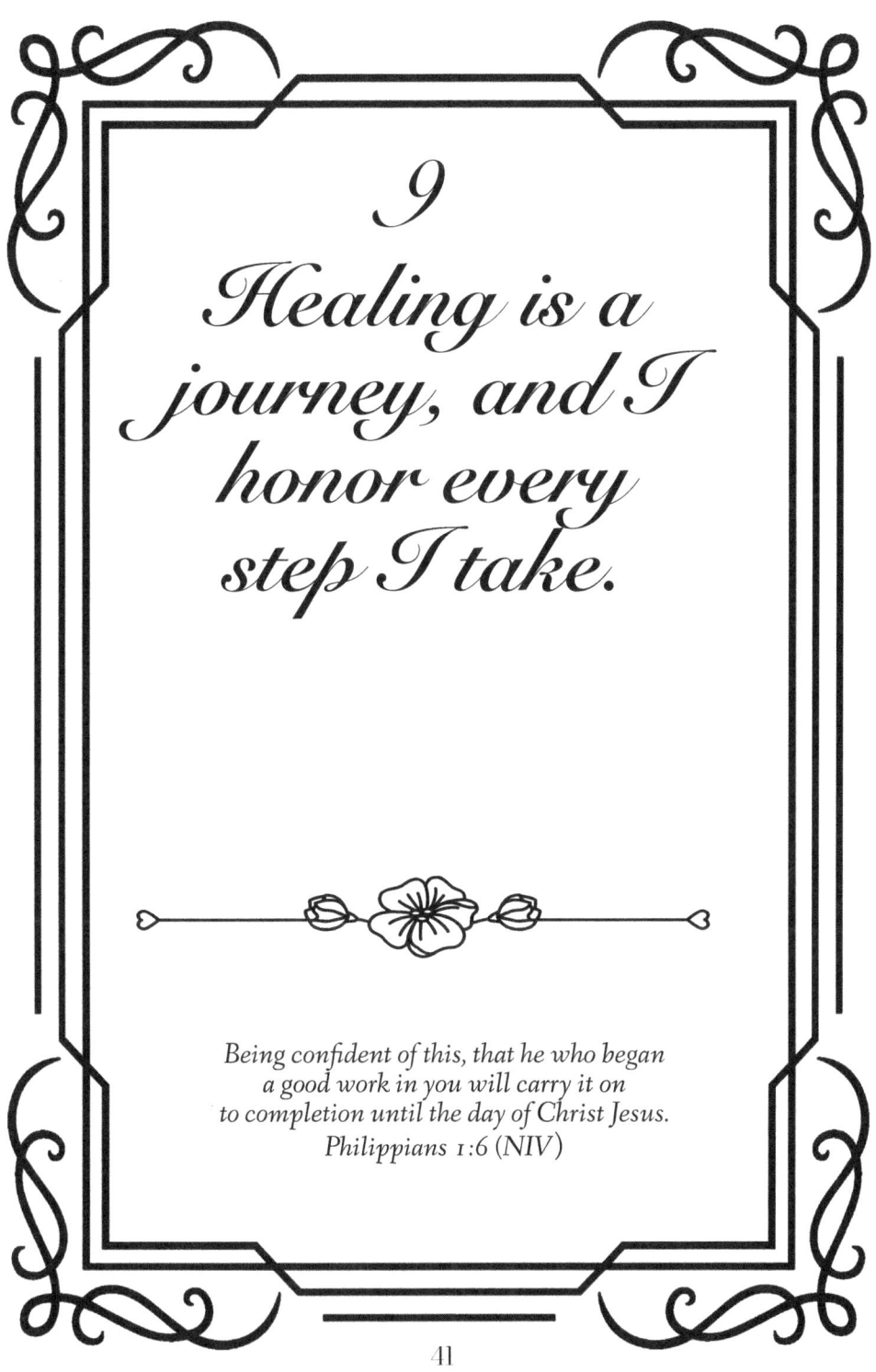

*Being confident of this, that he who began
a good work in you will carry it on
to completion until the day of Christ Jesus.
Philippians 1:6 (NIV)*

Reflection

Healing is not a journey we walk alone—God Himself carries us through. Philippians 1:6 assures us that the work He began in us—our growth, faith, and healing—will be completed in His perfect time.

Grief can feel endless, but God's hand is upon us, even in sorrow. The pain we carry is not wasted; it is part of His refining process, shaping us into something beautiful through our brokenness. The same God who gave us the capacity to love deeply is committed to restoring us.

Healing takes time, but God is always at work. Even when grief feels stagnant, He strengthens, comforts, and draws us closer to Him. The weight of loss will not last forever—our story is still unfolding, and His promise leads us toward renewal, wholeness, and peace.

A Prayer for Embracing the Healing Journey

Dear Lord,

Thank You for reminding me that healing is a process, not a destination. I trust that every step I take, no matter how small, is part of the work You are doing in my life. Help me to honor this journey, to be patient with myself, and to recognize the progress I am making.

When I feel discouraged or weary, remind me of Your promise to be with me always. Give me the strength to keep moving forward and the grace to accept where I am today. Fill me with hope for the future and peace in the present moment.

Thank You, Lord, for walking this journey with me and for gently guiding me toward wholeness. I trust in Your timing and in Your plan to bring beauty from my pain.

In Jesus' name, I pray,

Amen.

What step have you taken on your healing journey that you feel proud of?

_____
_____
_____
_____
_____
_____
_____
_____
_____
_____
_____
_____
_____

Today I feel

I will feel better tomorrow when I…

_____
_____
_____
_____
_____
_____
_____

I am grateful for…

_____
_____
_____
_____
_____
_____
_____
_____
_____
_____
_____
_____

Things to pray about…

_____
_____
_____
_____
_____
_____
_____

10

I release guilt and embrace peace within my heart.

So now there is no condemnation for those
who belong to Christ Jesus.
Romans 8:1 (NLT)

Reflection

Guilt has no hold on those who are in Christ. We are not bound by past mistakes, regrets, or the weight of self-condemnation—we are fully forgiven and fully loved.

For those grieving, guilt can be an unexpected companion. We may wrestle with what was left unsaid, moments of frustration, or even the ability to feel joy again. But Christ has already carried every burden, including our guilt. He does not condemn us for our emotions or the way we process loss; instead, He invites us into His peace.

This verse calls us to release the weight we were never meant to carry. Christ's sacrifice ensures that we are not defined by our failures but by His grace. In Him, we are free—free to grieve, to heal, and to live in the confidence of His unshakable love. His mercy is our refuge, and His peace is ours to embrace.

A Prayer for Releasing Guilt and Embracing Peace

Dear Lord,

Thank You for Your unconditional love and forgiveness. Today, I choose to release the guilt I have been carrying, knowing that it is not a burden You have asked me to bear. Help me to let go of any regret or self-blame, trusting in Your grace to heal my heart.

Fill the space once occupied by guilt with Your peace that surpasses all understanding. Remind me that I am human and that You are a God of second chances and new beginnings. Guide me to live with a heart free of shame, open to the joy and purpose You have for me.

Thank You, Lord, for Your mercy and for the promise of peace within my heart. I trust You to lead me forward in love and grace.

In Jesus' name, I pray,

Amen.

What guilt or burden are you ready to release to embrace peace in your heart?

_____
_____
_____
_____
_____
_____
_____
_____
_____
_____
_____
_____
_____

Today I feel

I will feel better tomorrow when I...

_____
_____
_____
_____
_____
_____

47

I am grateful for…

_____
_____
_____
_____
_____
_____
_____
_____
_____
_____
_____

Things to pray about…

_____
_____
_____
_____
_____
_____
_____

11

My grief is a reflection of my deep love, and that love will always remain.

Have I not commanded you? Be strong and courageous. Do not be afraid; do not be discouraged, for the Lord your God will be with you wherever you go.
Joshua 1:9 (NIV)

Reflection

While faith and hope sustain us, love is the greatest of all—it transcends time, circumstances, and even death. In grief, this truth offers deep comfort: the love we shared with those we've lost does not end. It remains within us, shaping our lives and guiding us forward.

Love is not diminished by loss. It lives on in our memories, our actions, and the ways we honor those who have gone before us. Whether through kindness, carrying forward their values, or cherishing their influence, love becomes their lasting legacy.

Even in sorrow, love is a healing force. It softens grief, offering strength and reassurance that we are never truly alone. God's love sustains us, surrounding us with comfort and the promise of renewal.

Paul's words in remind us in 1 Corinthians 13:13 that love is eternal, unbroken by earthly limitations. It connects us to our loved ones beyond this life, offering hope of reunion in God's presence. As we navigate loss, love remains our guide—an unshakable gift that carries us forward with peace, purpose, and enduring connection.

A Prayer for Grief and Love

Dear Lord,

Thank You for the gift of love that I was able to share with my loved one. Though my heart feels heavy with grief, I am reminded that it is a reflection of the deep love I hold for them. Help me to honor that love as something that will always remain, even as I continue to heal.

Lord, let my grief draw me closer to You, finding comfort in Your presence. Teach me to cherish the memories and lessons my loved one gave me and to carry their love in my heart as a source of strength and inspiration.

Thank You for Your promise that love never fades, and for holding me in Your embrace through my sorrow. Guide me as I navigate this journey, knowing that the love I feel is a testament to the beauty of the life we shared.

In Jesus' name, I pray,

Amen.

How does your grief reflect the deep love you hold, and how can you honor that love?

_____
_____
_____
_____
_____
_____
_____
_____
_____
_____
_____
_____
_____

Today I feel

I will feel better tomorrow when I...

_____
_____
_____
_____
_____
_____

I am grateful for…

_____

_____

_____

_____

_____

_____

_____

_____

_____

_____

_____

Things to pray about…

_____

_____

_____

_____

_____

_____

_____

12

The love I shared will always guide me toward hope and renewal.

"For I am convinced that neither death nor life,
neither angels nor demons, neither the present nor the future,
nor any powers, neither height nor depth, nor anything else in
all creation, will be able to separate us from the love of God
that is in Christ Jesus our Lord."
Romans 8:38-39 (NIV)

Reflection

Romans 8:38-39 declares a truth that brings deep comfort—nothing can separate us from God's love. Not life or death, not sorrow or uncertainty, not even the weight of grief. His love is constant, unshaken by time or circumstance, embracing us in every moment.

For those grieving, this promise is an anchor. Love does not end with loss—it endures, held securely in God's eternal embrace. The bond we shared with those we've lost remains, woven into the fabric of His unbreakable love.

When grief feels isolating, this verse reminds us that we are never alone. God's love sustains us in our lowest moments, offering strength when we feel weak and light when the path forward seems unclear. It meets us where we are and carries us through.

God's love is not just a comfort—it transforms. It ensures that grief does not consume us, renewing our hearts with hope and reminding us that His plan extends beyond what we can see. In His love, we find the strength to continue, to cherish the past, and to walk forward with faith, knowing that love—God's and our own—never truly ends.

A Prayer for Love and Renewal

Dear Lord,,
Thank You for the love I shared with my loved one, a gift that continues to guide me even now. Though they are no longer here with me, the love we shared is a source of strength and hope. Help me to draw from that love as I find renewal in each new day.

Lord, remind me that love is eternal and that it transcends all barriers, including loss. May this enduring love inspire me to live with purpose and grace, honoring their memory while embracing the future You have planned for me.

Thank You for Your presence in my journey and for showing me that love always points toward hope and renewal.

In Jesus' name, I pray,
Amen.

In what ways can the love you shared with your loved one guide you toward hope and renewal?

_____
_____
_____
_____
_____
_____
_____
_____
_____
_____
_____
_____

Today I feel

I will feel better tomorrow when I...

_____
_____
_____
_____
_____
_____

I am grateful for...

_____
_____
_____
_____
_____
_____
_____
_____
_____
_____
_____

Things to pray about...

_____
_____
_____
_____
_____
_____

13

I am creating a future that honors my past while embracing new opportunities.

Forget the former things; do not dwell on the past.
See, I am doing a new thing! Now it springs up; do
you not perceive it? I am making a way in the
wilderness and streams in the wasteland.
Isaiah 43:18-19 (NIV)

Reflection

Isaiah 43:18-19 reminds us that while the past is worth honoring, God is always at work bringing renewal and new beginnings. Forgetting former things doesn't mean erasing the past but refusing to be trapped by it. Grief naturally ties us to what we've lost, yet God gently calls us to move forward, trusting that He is not finished with our story.

Even in sorrow, God is doing something new. Loss may feel like the end, but God specializes in bringing life from brokenness. Just as streams refresh the desert, His presence breathes hope into the empty places in our hearts. Even when we can't see it, He is working behind the scenes, creating something beautiful in His perfect timing.

Healing and renewal take time, often unfolding in ways we don't immediately recognize. A moment of peace, an unexpected opportunity, a renewed sense of purpose—these are glimpses of the "new thing" God is doing. When grief clouds our vision, this verse reminds us to trust His process, knowing that no situation is too barren for Him to transform.

God's grace flows like streams in the wilderness, sustaining and guiding us toward renewal. His work in our lives is ongoing, leading us not to dwell in loss but to step forward with faith. He is making a way—even when we can't yet see the path—calling us into a future filled with hope, healing, and His unending love.

A Prayer for Honoring the Past and Embracing the Future

Dear Lord,
Thank You for the strength and wisdom to honor my past while stepping into the new opportunities You have placed before me. Help me to carry the love and lessons from my journey as I create a future that reflects both growth and grace.

Guide me to trust in Your plan, knowing that my past has shaped me, but it does not limit the possibilities You have for me. Open my heart to embrace change with faith and courage, and let my actions honor the memories and the blessings I hold dear.

Thank You, Lord, for being my foundation and my guide as I move forward. I trust that You are with me every step of the way.

In Jesus' name, I pray,
Amen.

How can you create a future that honors your past while embracing new opportunities?

_____
_____
_____
_____
_____
_____
_____
_____
_____
_____
_____
_____
_____

Today I feel

I will feel better tomorrow when I…

_____
_____
_____
_____
_____
_____

I am grateful for...

_____
_____
_____
_____
_____
_____
_____
_____
_____
_____
_____
_____

Things to pray about...

_____
_____
_____
_____
_____
_____
_____

14

I carry my loved one's memory in my heart, where they will always live.

The memory of the righteous is a blessing.
Proverbs 10:7 (NIV)

Reflection

"The memory of the righteous is a blessing" (Proverbs 10:7) reminds us that the love, wisdom, and kindness of those we cherish do not fade with their passing. Their lives leave an imprint that continues to shape and inspire us.

In grief, their memory becomes a source of comfort—not just a reflection of the past, but a guiding light for the future. A shared laugh, a cherished tradition, or a lesson they instilled reminds us that their presence is still felt, woven into the fabric of our lives.

Honoring their legacy means carrying forward the values they lived by—kindness, faith, and integrity—so their impact continues to ripple outward. Their influence is not lost; it lives on in us.

God, in His grace, gives us the gift of memory—not just to remember, but to feel connected, uplifted, and strengthened. Through our love and actions, their story continues, a blessing that never fades.

A Prayer for Cherished Memories

Dear Lord,

Thank You for the gift of memory and for the love I carry in my heart. Though my loved one is no longer with me, their presence remains alive through the memories we created together. These moments bring me comfort and strength, reminding me of the beauty and love that we shared.

Help me to honor their memory in the way I live my life, letting their influence guide me toward kindness, purpose, and joy. May these cherished memories be a source of peace and a reminder that love transcends all barriers.

Thank You, Lord, for Your constant presence and for holding me close as I carry my loved one's memory with me.

In Jesus' name, I pray,

Amen.

What memory of your loved one do you carry in your heart, and how does it bring you comfort?

_____
_____
_____
_____
_____
_____
_____
_____
_____
_____
_____
_____

Today I feel

I will feel better tomorrow when I…

_____
_____
_____
_____
_____
_____
_____

I am grateful for…

_____
_____
_____
_____
_____
_____
_____
_____
_____
_____
_____
_____
_____

Things to pray about…

_____
_____
_____
_____
_____
_____
_____
_____

15

I find comfort in the support of others who care for me.

Carry each other's burdens, and in this way,
you will fulfill the law of Christ.
Galatians 6:2 (NIV)

Reflection

We are not meant to face struggles alone. Instead, God calls us to support one another, reflecting Christ's love through our actions. Life can often feel overwhelming. Grief, loss, and hardships can weigh us down, making it difficult to move forward on our own. This verse encourages us to lean on one another, allowing others to help carry the weight of our struggles while being willing to do the same for them.

There is healing power in community. In times of grief, it's easy to feel isolated, as though no one can truly understand what we are going through. Yet, Galatians 6:2 reminds us that God created us to live in connection with others. Sharing our burdens with trusted friends, family, or a faith community allows us to experience the love and support we need to heal. At the same time, supporting others in their struggles can be equally transformative. When we step into someone else's pain with compassion, we not only help them but also grow in our own faith and character. In this mutual exchange of care, community becomes a sacred space where God's love is made tangible.

It's okay to seek and accept help. Grief is a heavy burden, and God often provides comfort and strength through the care of others. Shared prayers, words of encouragement, or practical acts of kindness can make the journey through loss more bearable. At the same time, Galatians 6:2 reminds us of the blessing of being there for others who are hurting. Offering support, even in small ways, allows us to be part of God's work in their lives. It is a reminder that love and care are powerful tools for healing, both for those who give and those who receive.

We are stronger together. Through shared burdens, we reflect Christ's love, find comfort in community, and help one another experience God's grace in the midst of life's challenges.

A Prayer for Comfort and Support

Dear Lord,

Thank You for placing people in my life who care for me and offer their support. Their kindness and presence remind me that I am not alone, even in my moments of deepest sorrow. Help me to find comfort in their love and to recognize it as a reflection of Your care for me.

Teach me to be open to the encouragement and help of others, and guide me to be a source of love and comfort in return. May their support strengthen my spirit and remind me of the beauty of connection and community.

Thank You for surrounding me with the love of others and for always being near to my heart.

In Jesus' name, I pray,

Amen.

Who has offered you support, and how can you lean into that care for comfort and strength?

_____
_____
_____
_____
_____
_____
_____
_____
_____
_____
_____
_____

Today I feel

I will feel better tomorrow when I…

_____
_____
_____
_____
_____
_____
_____

I am grateful for...

_____
_____
_____
_____
_____
_____
_____
_____
_____
_____
_____
_____

Things to pray about...

_____
_____
_____
_____
_____
_____
_____

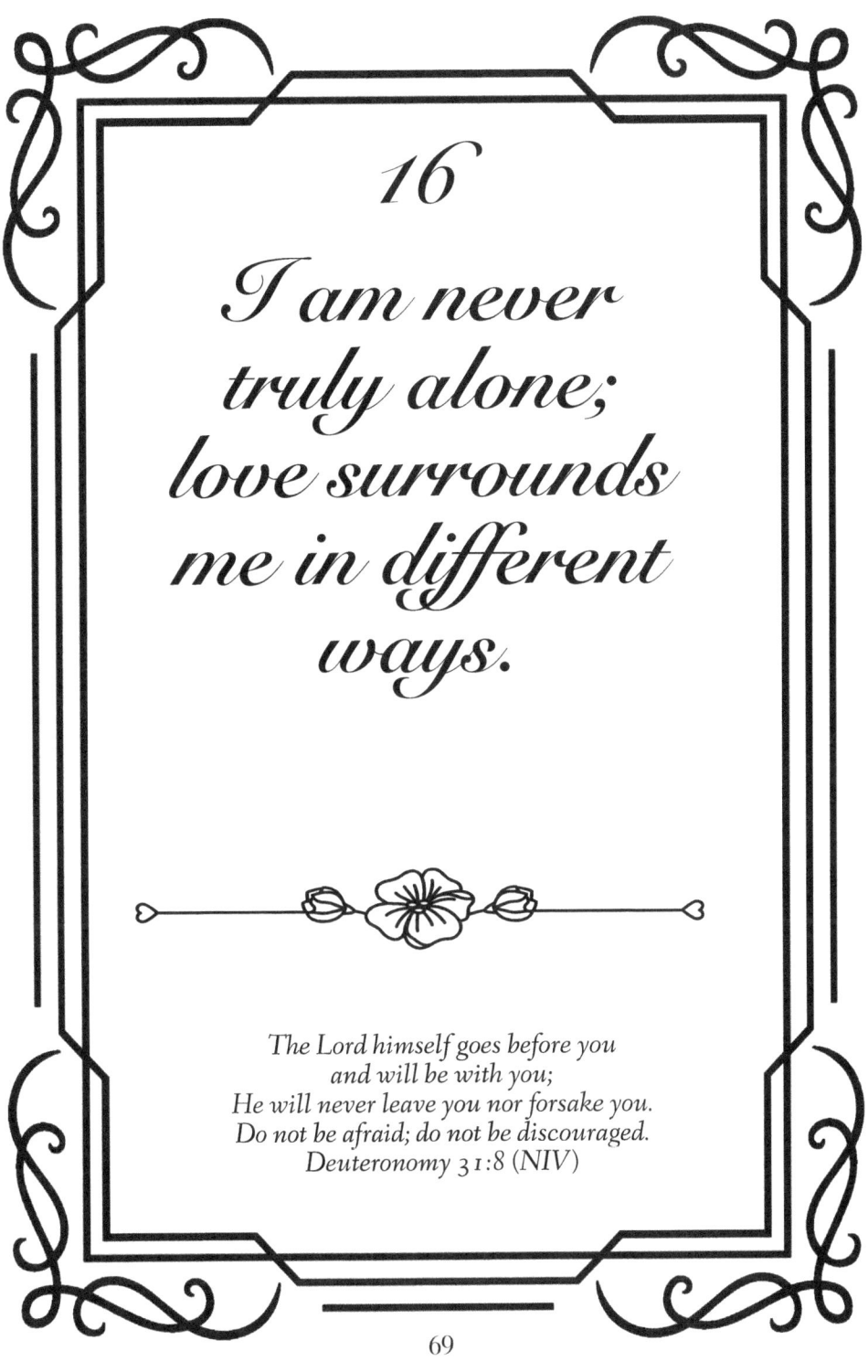

16

I am never truly alone; love surrounds me in different ways.

The Lord himself goes before you
and will be with you;
He will never leave you nor forsake you.
Do not be afraid; do not be discouraged.
Deuteronomy 31:8 (NIV)

Reflection

Grief can feel like uncharted territory—overwhelming, uncertain, and exhausting. Joshua 1:9 assures us that we are not meant to walk this path alone. God's presence is our anchor, offering strength when ours feels depleted and courage when fear takes hold.

This call to be strong is not about suppressing pain but about trusting that God walks with us, even in our brokenness. It takes courage to face each day, to grieve fully, and to believe in healing. Yet, God's promise remains: He goes before us, beside us, and carries us through.

On the hardest days, when discouragement sets in, He provides more than a command—He provides Himself. His presence renews our strength, His peace calms our fear, and His love fills the emptiness. We do not have to rely on our own strength; we are held by the One who never leaves us. With Him, we can keep moving forward, step by step, toward hope and healing.

A Prayer for Strength and Courage

Dear Lord,

Thank You for being my refuge and source of strength. In moments when I feel weak and overwhelmed, remind me of the courage You have placed within me. Help me to trust in Your power to sustain me and guide me through every challenge I face.

Give me the faith to take each day one step at a time, knowing that You are always by my side. When my spirit feels weary, renew my strength, and when my heart feels heavy, lift my burdens.

Lord, I declare that with Your help, I am stronger than I feel. Fill me with peace and boldness to face the unknown, confident in Your promises and love. Thank You for walking this journey with me and for the courage You provide each day.

In Jesus' name, I pray,

Amen

How have you felt love surrounding you, even in unexpected ways?

_____
_____
_____
_____
_____
_____
_____
_____
_____
_____
_____
_____

Today I feel

😊 🙄

😭 😢

I will feel better tomorrow when I…

_____
_____
_____
_____
_____
_____

I am grateful for…

_____
_____
_____
_____
_____
_____
_____
_____
_____
_____
_____
_____

Things to pray about…

_____
_____
_____
_____
_____
_____
_____

17

I am deeply loved, and I love deeply in return.

And so we know and rely on the love God has for us. God is love. Whoever lives in love lives in God, and God in them.
1 John 4:16 (NIV)

Reflection

God's love is not just something He gives; it is who He is. His love is constant, unshaken by circumstances, and the foundation upon which we can build our lives.

In grief and hardship, this love sustains us. It is not conditional or earned; it surrounds us, offering comfort when we feel lost and strength when we feel weak. Even when we struggle to see our worth, God's love remains, reminding us that we are deeply cherished.

To live in God's love is to trust in its power—to let it shape our hearts, guide our relationships, and inspire us to extend kindness and grace to others. It frees us from seeking validation elsewhere, grounding us in the assurance that we are fully known and fully loved.

For those mourning a loss, this truth is especially comforting. God's love fills the spaces left by grief, holding us close and leading us toward healing. It transforms pain into purpose, sorrow into hope, and reminds us that love—His and ours—never truly fades.

1 John 4:16 is more than a promise; it is an invitation. To embrace God's love is to live in its fullness, allowing it to restore, renew, and radiate through us. In every season of life, His love is our anchor, our strength, and our greatest gift.

A Prayer for Love and Gratitude

Dear Lord,

Thank You for the gift of love that flows through my life. I am deeply loved by You and by those You have placed in my life, and I am grateful for the opportunity to love deeply in return. Help me to cherish this love as a reflection of Your grace and a source of strength and joy.

Teach me to express love freely and to receive it with an open heart. Let my love inspire and uplift others, and may I always be reminded of the infinite love You have for me.

Thank You for surrounding me with Your love and for teaching me how to share it with others.

In Jesus' name, I pray,

Amen.

In what ways do you give and receive love deeply in your life?

_____
_____
_____
_____
_____
_____
_____
_____
_____
_____
_____
_____

Today I feel

I will feel better tomorrow when I…

_____
_____
_____
_____
_____
_____

I am grateful for…

_____
_____
_____
_____
_____
_____
_____
_____
_____
_____
_____

Things to pray about…

_____
_____
_____
_____
_____
_____
_____

18

I trust myself to make decisions that are best for me and my healing.

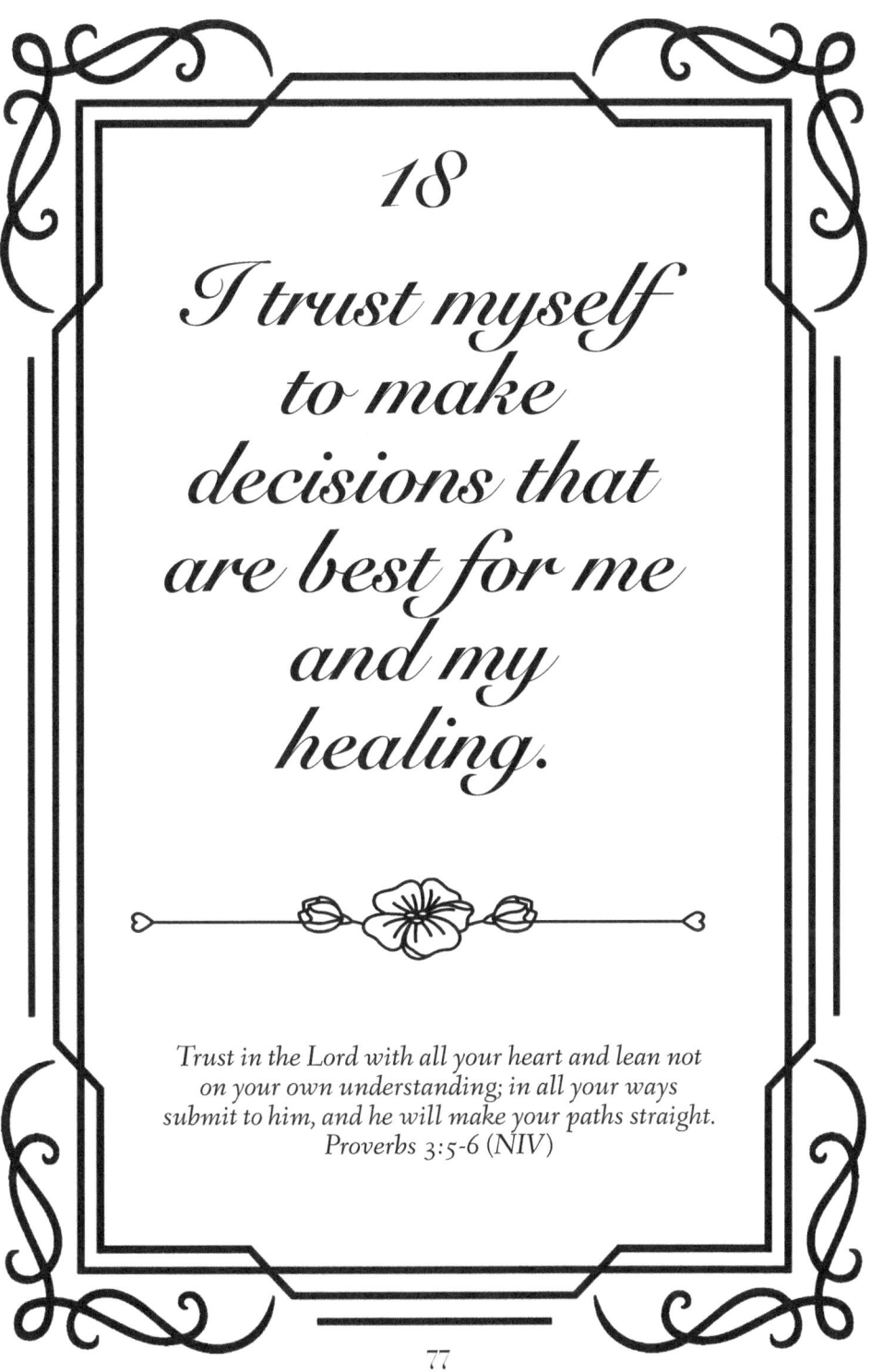

Trust in the Lord with all your heart and lean not on your own understanding; in all your ways submit to him, and he will make your paths straight.
Proverbs 3:5-6 (NIV)

Reflection

Losing a loved one can leave us feeling lost, searching for stability in the midst of sorrow. Proverbs 3:5-6 calls us to trust in God—not because grief is easy, but because He is faithful even when life feels uncertain.

Grief brings questions with no easy answers. Trusting God doesn't mean ignoring our pain but bringing it to Him, knowing He walks with us through it. We don't have to figure everything out on our own—His wisdom is greater than ours, and His love sustains us even when we don't understand the "why."

Surrendering our grief to God isn't about rushing healing but allowing Him to guide our steps. He clears a path, even in the wilderness of loss, leading us toward peace, renewal, and purpose. The road may not be easy, but He promises to make it straight—aligning our journey with His greater plan.

This verse offers hope: grief is not a destination, but a journey God is leading us through. Trusting Him allows us to move forward without fear, resting in the promise that He is with us, making a way toward healing, hope, and new beginnings.

A Prayer for Trust and Discernment

Dear Lord,

Thank You for the wisdom and strength You have given me. I trust myself, with Your guidance, to make decisions that are best for my healing and well-being. Help me to listen to the quiet voice of Your Spirit within me and to act with clarity and confidence.

Grant me discernment to know what choices align with the path You have prepared for me. Teach me to honor my needs and to embrace decisions that nurture my growth and bring me closer to the peace and wholeness You desire for me.

Thank You for walking with me every step of the way and for filling me with the courage to trust in myself and in Your plan.

In Jesus' name, I pray,

Amen.

What decision have you made recently that has supported your healing journey?

_____
_____
_____
_____
_____
_____
_____
_____
_____
_____
_____
_____

Today I feel

I will feel better tomorrow when I...

_____
_____
_____
_____
_____
_____

I am grateful for...

_____
_____
_____
_____
_____
_____
_____
_____
_____
_____
_____

Things to pray about...

_____
_____
_____
_____
_____
_____
_____

19

I am not defined by my loss but by my courage to keep moving forward.

Consider it pure joy, my brothers and sisters,
whenever you face trials of many kinds, because you know that
the testing of your faith produces perseverance. Let
perseverance finish its work so that you may be mature and
complete, not lacking anything.
James 1:2-4

Reflection

Grief shakes our foundations, leaving us vulnerable and searching for meaning. James 1:2-4 challenges us to see trials—including the deep sorrow of loss—not as meaningless suffering but as opportunities for growth. Perseverance, shaped by faith, refines us and strengthens our spirit.

Finding joy in grief may seem impossible, but James is not asking us to celebrate pain. Instead, he calls us to embrace how God works within us during sorrow, molding us into a deeper reflection of His love and grace. Grief strips away self-sufficiency, drawing us closer to God's strength. Perseverance is not passive; it is an act of trust—believing that even in heartbreak, God is leading us toward healing.

Through endurance, we learn to carry sorrow and joy together. We become more compassionate, resilient, and spiritually mature. Though grief is heavy, it is not without purpose. God is using even our hardest moments to shape us, ensuring that, in time, we emerge stronger, more whole, and deeply rooted in His love.

A Prayer for Strength and Courage

Dear Lord,

Thank You for reminding me that I am not defined by my loss but by the courage You give me to keep moving forward. Help me to see myself through Your eyes, as someone strong, capable, and resilient.

When the weight of grief feels overwhelming, remind me that my story is not one of despair but of hope and perseverance. Teach me to embrace each new day as an opportunity to grow, to heal, and to step closer to the purpose You have for my life.

Thank You, Lord, for walking this journey with me and for being my constant source of strength and courage.

In Jesus' name, I pray,

Amen.

How do you define yourself beyond your loss, and what courage have you shown in moving forward?

_____
_____
_____
_____
_____
_____
_____
_____
_____
_____
_____
_____
_____

Today I feel

I will feel better tomorrow when I...

_____
_____
_____
_____
_____
_____

I am grateful for...

_____
_____
_____
_____
_____
_____
_____
_____
_____
_____
_____
_____
_____

Things to pray about...

_____
_____
_____
_____
_____
_____
_____
_____

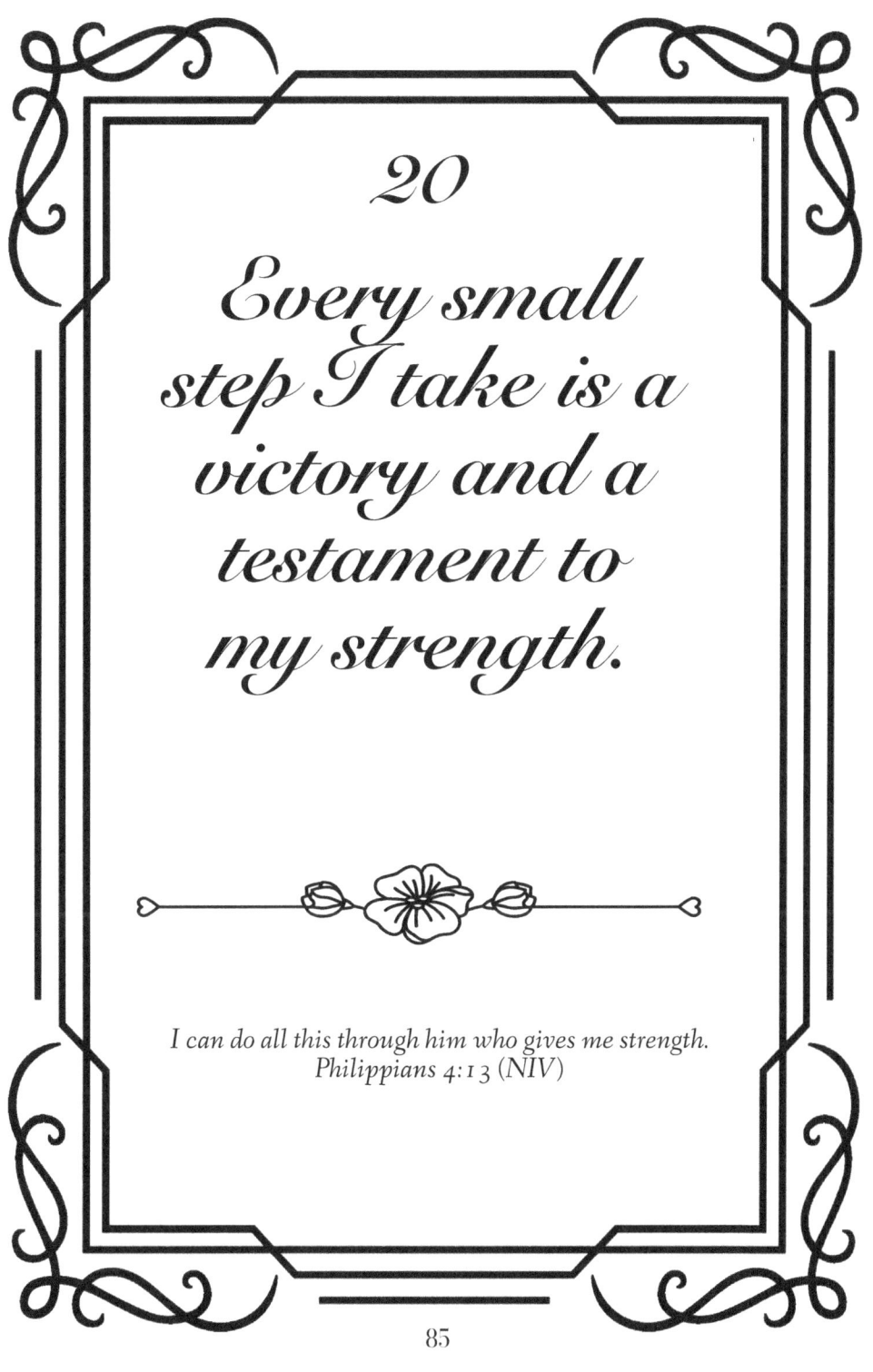

20

Every small step I take is a victory and a testament to my strength.

I can do all this through him who gives me strength.
Philippians 4:13 (NIV)

Reflection

Philippians 4:13 is a powerful declaration that our ability to move forward—especially through grief—is not dependent on our own strength but on Christ's. Paul, writing from prison, speaks not of personal ambition but of God's sufficiency in every season, whether in abundance or need.

Grief can feel like an impossible weight, but this verse reminds us that every step—no matter how small—is made possible through God's strength. Facing another day, confronting painful emotions, or rediscovering hope is not something we do alone. His presence sustains us, lifting us when we feel weak and guiding us toward renewal.

God's strength is not about rushing healing but equipping us to endure. Each moment of courage, each step forward, is a testament to His power at work within us. Even in sorrow, we are not alone. With Him, we can keep moving, keep believing, and keep trusting that hope and healing are ahead.

A Prayer for Celebrating Small Victories

Dear Lord,
Thank You for the strength You give me each day to take even the smallest steps forward. Remind me that every step, no matter how small, is a victory and a testament to the resilience You have placed within me.

Help me to recognize and celebrate my progress, knowing that healing is a journey and not a race. Encourage me to keep moving forward with faith, trusting that You are guiding me every step of the way.

Thank You, Lord, for being my source of strength and for rejoicing with me in every step I take.

In Jesus' name, I pray,
Amen.

What small victory did you achieve today that demonstrates your strength?

_____
_____
_____
_____
_____
_____
_____
_____
_____
_____
_____
_____

Today I feel

I will feel better tomorrow when I...

_____
_____
_____
_____
_____
_____

I am grateful for…

_____
_____
_____
_____
_____
_____
_____
_____
_____
_____
_____

Things to pray about…

_____
_____
_____
_____
_____
_____
_____

21

My strength grows deeper each day.

But he said to me, 'My grace is sufficient for you, for my power is made perfect in weakness.' Therefore I will boast all the more gladly about my weaknesses, so that Christ's power may rest on me. That is why, for Christ's sake, I delight in weaknesses, in insults, in hardships, in persecutions, in difficulties.
For when I am weak, then I am strong.
2 Corinthians 12:9-10 (NIV)

Reflection

2 Corinthians 12:9-10 reveals a powerful truth—true strength is not found in self-sufficiency but in dependence on God. His grace is not just enough to sustain us; it is the very source of strength that grows within us, especially in our weakest moments.

Paul's words challenge the world's definition of strength. While we often equate strength with control, God calls us to embrace our limitations and lean on Him. In grief and hardship, when we feel depleted, His power sustains us. Each day, as we surrender our struggles, He strengthens us in ways unseen but deeply felt.

God's grace transforms weakness into resilience. Every challenge becomes an opportunity to trust Him more, deepening our faith and shaping us into people who walk with confidence—not in our own ability, but in His unwavering power.

Our weaknesses are not barriers but openings for God's strength to shine through. The more we rely on Him, the deeper our strength grows. Each day is an invitation to trust, to rest in His grace, and to live with renewed faith, knowing that His power is made perfect in our weakness.

A Prayer for Growing Strength

Dear Lord,

Thank You for the strength You provide me every day. I feel my strength growing deeper with each challenge I face and each step I take on this journey. Help me to trust in Your power to sustain me and to guide me toward wholeness.

When I feel weary, remind me of how far I have already come and of the resilience You have built within me. May my growing strength be a reflection of Your grace and a testament to Your faithfulness in my life.

Thank You, Lord, for walking with me and for renewing my spirit daily.

In Jesus' name, I pray,

Amen.

How has your strength grown over time, and what helps you feel stronger each day?

_____

_____

_____

_____

_____

_____

_____

_____

_____

_____

_____

_____

_____

_____

Today I feel

I will feel better tomorrow when I...

_____

_____

_____

_____

_____

_____

I am grateful for…

_____
_____
_____
_____
_____
_____
_____
_____
_____
_____
_____
_____

Things to pray about…

_____
_____
_____
_____
_____
_____
_____

22

I honor my grief while embracing possibilities.

To provide for those who grieve in Zion—to bestow on them a crown of beauty instead of ashes, the oil of joy instead of mourning, and a garment of praise instead of a spirit of despair. They will be called oaks of righteousness, a planting of the Lord
for the display of his splendor.
Isaiah 61:3 (NIV)

Reflection

Grief can feel like an unshakable weight, a season of sorrow that seems endless. Yet, even in our darkest moments, God is at work, bringing beauty from ashes and turning despair into praise. He does not erase pain but transforms it, offering renewal and purpose beyond our loss.

Mourning is honored, not dismissed. Healing does not mean forgetting, but rather allowing God to restore what feels broken. He replaces heaviness with joy, guiding us toward a future where hope and celebration coexist with the love we carry from the past.

Like oaks of righteousness, we are strengthened and deeply rooted in His promises. Grief may shake us, but it does not define us—through God's grace, we emerge resilient, standing as a testimony to His faithfulness. Isaiah 61:3 is an invitation to trust the journey, to embrace both sorrow and renewal, and to believe that even in loss, God is creating something beautiful.

A Prayer for Honoring Grief and Embracing Possibilities

Dear Lord,

Thank You for walking with me through my grief and for opening my heart to the possibilities ahead. Help me to honor the sadness I feel, knowing it is a reflection of love, while also embracing the hope and opportunities You have prepared for me.

Guide me to find balance as I navigate this journey, carrying my memories with grace while stepping forward in faith. Teach me to trust that You can bring beauty from my pain and lead me to a future filled with promise.

Thank You, Lord, for Your constant presence and for giving me the courage to embrace both grief and new beginnings.

In Jesus' name, I pray,

Amen.

How can you honor your grief while staying open to new possibilities?

_____
_____
_____
_____
_____
_____
_____
_____
_____
_____
_____
_____

Today I feel

I will feel better tomorrow when I…

_____
_____
_____
_____
_____

I am grateful for...

Things to pray about...

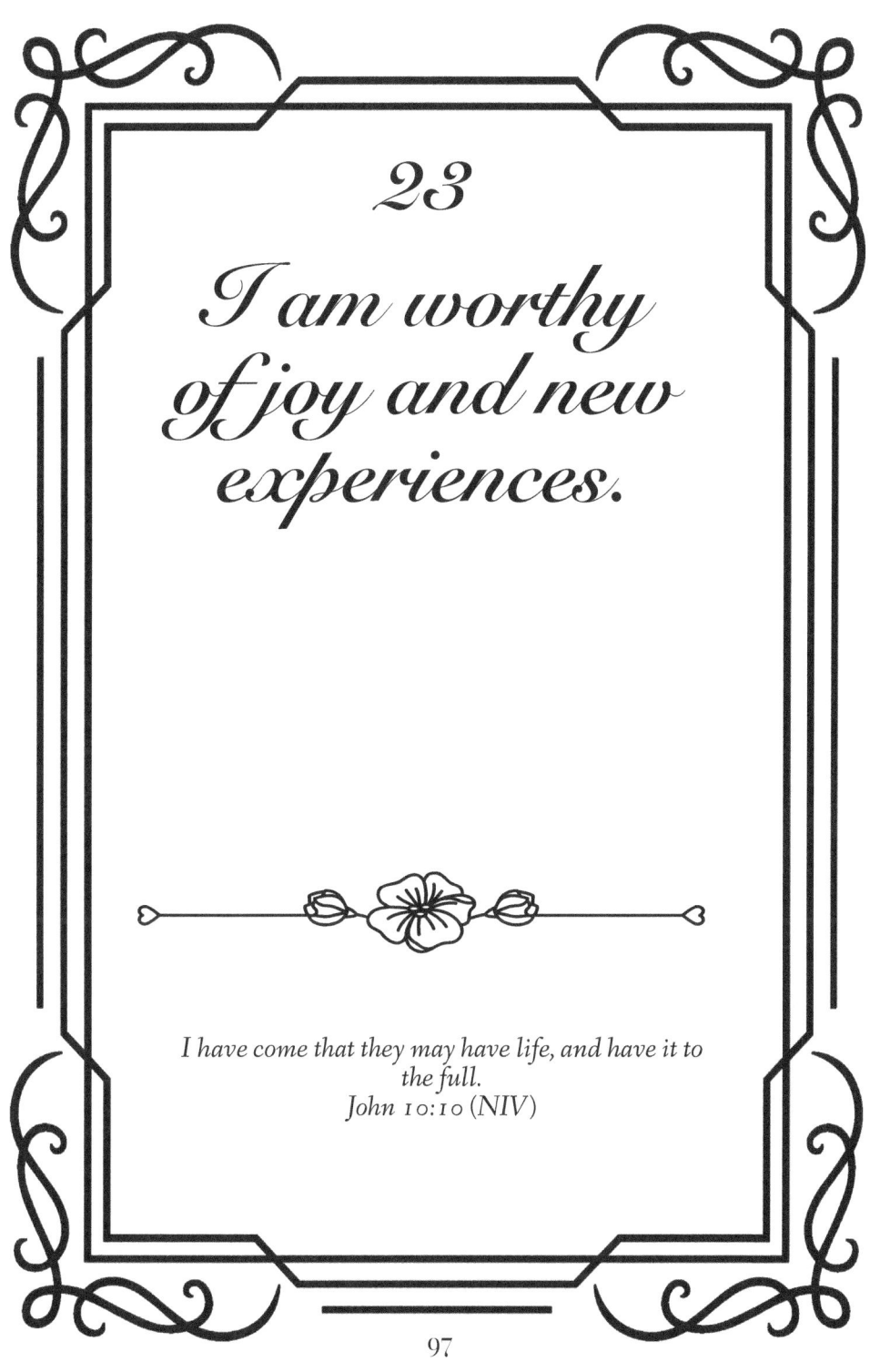

23

I am worthy of joy and new experiences.

I have come that they may have life, and have it to the full.
John 10:10 (NIV)

Reflection

Grief can feel like it drains life of its meaning, leaving behind emptiness, loneliness, and sorrow. Yet, even in our pain, Jesus invites us into a life of abundance—not in material wealth, but in the depth of His peace, comfort, and presence. He does not ask us to ignore our grief but to walk through it with Him, trusting that even in loss, life can still hold love, purpose, and hope.

John 10:10 reminds us that Jesus came so that we may have life and have it to the full. Living fully after loss means allowing Him to fill the broken spaces of our hearts with His sustaining grace. It means honoring what we have lost while remaining open to the beauty and blessings still ahead. Grief does not define our entire story—Jesus does.

Even in sorrow, there are moments of grace: the warmth of a cherished memory, the kindness of others, the quiet reassurance of God's presence. He is always working to bring renewal, guiding us toward healing and a future still rich with His love. Life, even after loss, is still abundant when lived in Him.

A Prayer for Worthiness and Renewal

Dear Lord,

Thank You for creating me in Your image and for reminding me that I am worthy of joy and new experiences. Help me to let go of any doubts or fears that hold me back and to embrace the abundant life You have planned for me.

Open my heart to receive the blessings You provide and to seek joy in the opportunities that come my way. Teach me to walk confidently in the knowledge that I am loved, cherished, and deserving of all the good things You have in store.

Thank You, Lord, for filling my life with possibilities and for calling me to live with hope and purpose.

In Jesus' name, I pray,

Amen.

What brings you joy, and how can you create more joyful experiences in your life?

_____
_____
_____
_____
_____
_____
_____
_____
_____
_____
_____
_____

Today I feel

I will feel better tomorrow when I…

_____
_____
_____
_____
_____

I am grateful for...

Things to pray about...

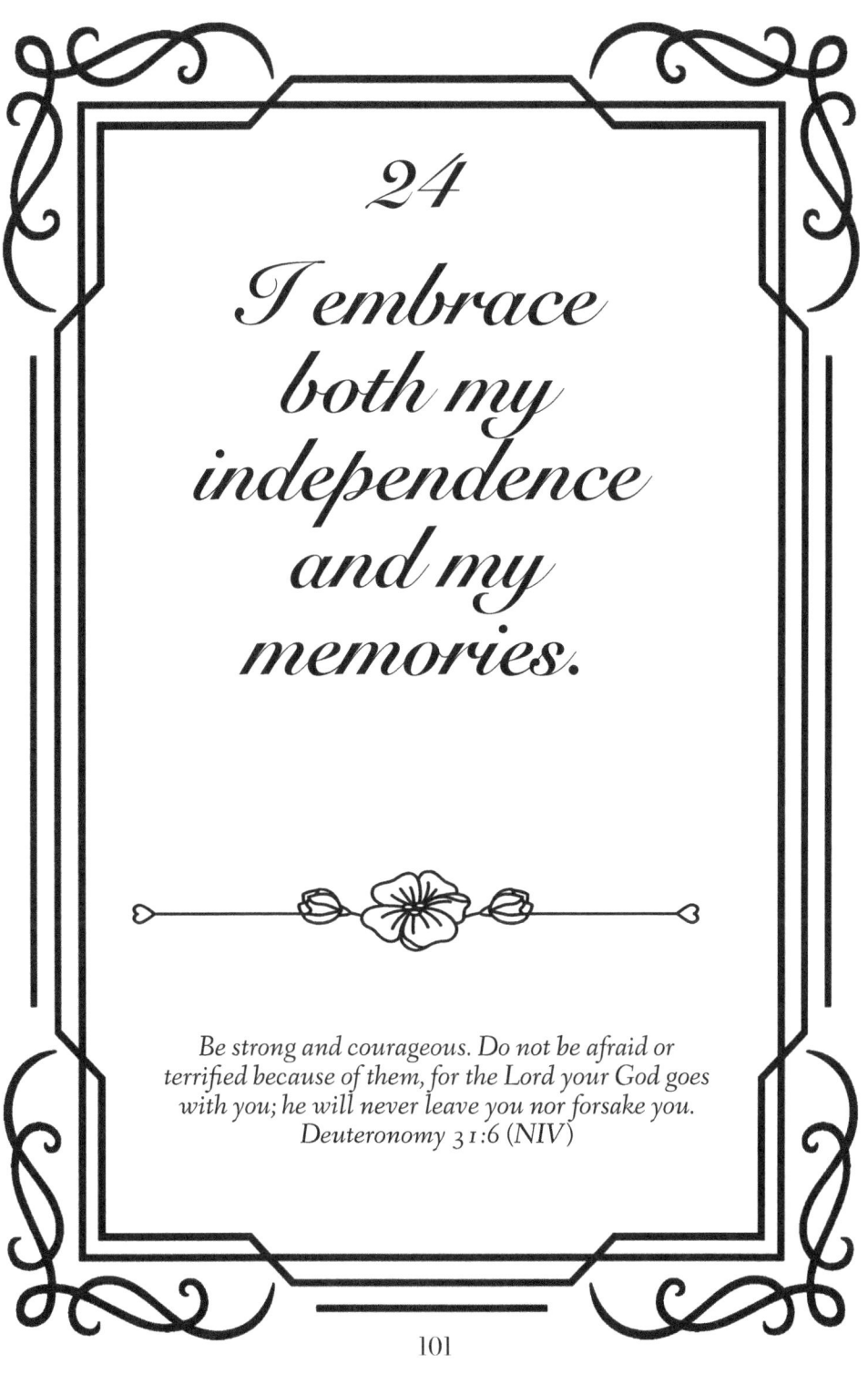

24

I embrace both my independence and my memories.

Be strong and courageous. Do not be afraid or terrified because of them, for the Lord your God goes with you; he will never leave you nor forsake you.
Deuteronomy 31:6 (NIV)

Reflection

Grief can feel like uncharted territory—overwhelming, uncertain, and exhausting. Jo

Grief is a journey that calls us to walk forward while carrying the love and memories of those who have passed. It is a delicate balance—learning to stand on our own while holding onto the moments that shaped us. In times of sorrow, it may feel as though we are alone, navigating uncharted waters without the comfort of the familiar. Yet, God assures us that we are never truly by ourselves.

Deuteronomy 31:6 reminds us, "Be strong and courageous. Do not be afraid or terrified because of them, for the Lord your God goes with you; he will never leave you nor forsake you." Even in the depths of grief, when loneliness presses in, we are not abandoned. The same God who has been with us in joy remains with us in sorrow.

Embracing independence in grief does not mean forgetting or leaving behind the love we once shared. Rather, it is stepping forward with faith, trusting that God is walking beside us, strengthening us when we feel weak. He calls us to be courageous—to face each new day with the assurance that His presence will sustain us.

At the same time, our memories serve as sacred reminders of the love that continues beyond death. They are not meant to chain us to the past but to encourage us, to comfort us, and to remind us of God's faithfulness through every season. Just as Israel was reminded to remember God's works and trust in His guidance, we too are called to hold onto the blessings of the past while stepping into the future with confidence.

Grief does not mean choosing between remembering and moving forward. It is the blending of both—the courage to embrace life anew while treasuring the love that remains. And in every step, God is with us, never leaving, never forsaking, carrying us through with His unwavering strength.

A Prayer for Independence and Cherished Memories

Dear Lord,

Thank You for the strength to embrace my independence while holding onto the precious memories of my loved one. Help me to navigate this balance with grace, honoring the past while confidently stepping into the future You have for me.

Teach me to lean on the lessons and love that shaped me while discovering the courage to stand on my own. May I find peace in knowing that my memories will always be a part of me, guiding me as I grow and move forward.

Thank You, Lord, for being my constant source of strength and for helping me embrace both independence and the love that endures in my heart.

In Jesus' name, I pray,

Amen.

How do you balance independence with cherishing your memories?

_____
_____
_____
_____
_____
_____
_____
_____
_____
_____
_____
_____

Today I feel

I will feel better tomorrow when I...

_____
_____
_____
_____
_____

I am grateful for...

Things to pray about...

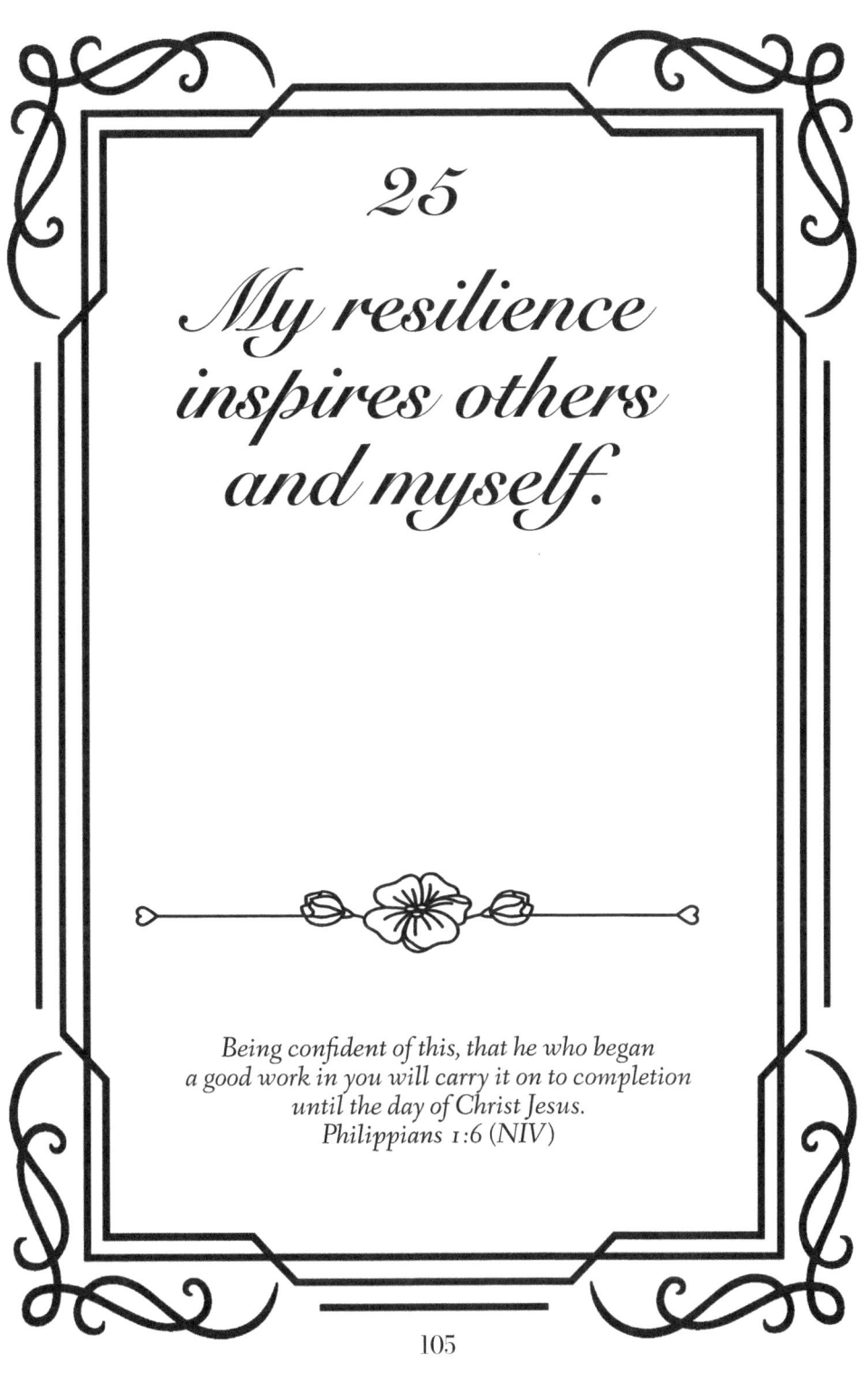

25

My resilience inspires others and myself.

*Being confident of this, that he who began
a good work in you will carry it on to completion
until the day of Christ Jesus.
Philippians 1:6 (NIV)*

Reflection

Grief can make it difficult to see beyond the pain, but even in sorrow, God is actively working in us. The healing, growth, and resilience that emerge through grief are all part of the "good work" He has begun, shaping us into something new.

Philippians 1:6 assures us that grief is not a permanent state but a part of God's process of restoration. Though the journey may feel overwhelming, He is guiding us step by step, strengthening our hearts and preparing us for new seasons filled with meaning and purpose.

Even when grief brings doubt or uncertainty, we can trust in God's faithfulness. The healing process may be slow, but He will never abandon us. His work in us is ongoing, leading us toward hope and wholeness.

This verse also reminds us that our journey can bring encouragement to others. As we grow in resilience, the strength and comfort God builds within us can inspire others to trust in His presence and promises.

Grief is not the end of the story. God's work continues through the tears and heartache, shaping us into stronger, more compassionate people who reflect His love. Trusting this promise allows us to face sorrow with courage, knowing that His plan is one of healing, renewal, and completion.

A Prayer for Resilience and Inspiration

Dear Lord,

Thank You for the resilience You have placed within me, a strength that not only helps me overcome challenges but also inspires those around me. Help me to see the impact of my perseverance, both in my own life and in the lives of others who may draw courage from my journey.

Guide me to continue growing in resilience, knowing that it is a reflection of Your grace and faithfulness. May my strength be a testimony to the power of hope, and may it encourage others to trust in Your love and provision.

Thank You, Lord, for making me an example of resilience and for using my journey to bring hope to myself and those I encounter.

In Jesus' name, I pray,

Amen.

How has your resilience inspired both yourself and others around you?

_____

_____

_____

_____

_____

_____

_____

_____

_____

_____

_____

_____

_____

Today I feel

I will feel better tomorrow when I...

_____

_____

_____

_____

_____

I am grateful for...

Things to pray about...

26

I give myself permission to laugh and find happiness.

*Our mouths were filled with laughter, our tongues
with songs of joy. Then it was said among the
nations, 'The Lord has done great things for them.'*
Psalm 126:2 (NIV)

Reflection

Joy has a way of breaking through even the heaviest seasons, and when it does, it is a testament to God's faithfulness. Psalm 126:2 paints a vivid picture of hearts overflowing with laughter and voices lifted in gratitude—a moment where sorrow is transformed into celebration.

This joy is not fleeting or shallow; it is rooted in the deep recognition of God's goodness. It is the kind of joy that others notice, prompting them to say, "The Lord has done great things for them." Our laughter and songs of praise become a reflection of His power to restore, heal, and bless.

Joy is not the absence of hardship but the presence of God's blessings. Even in seasons of transition or healing, moments of happiness serve as glimpses of His ongoing work in our lives. Embracing gratitude opens our hearts to even more joy, reminding us that God is always at work, shaping a story that will one day be filled with laughter and praise.

This verse invites us to celebrate the beauty of life—to recognize joy as a sacred gift, a reflection of God's love, and a promise of the restoration yet to come.

A Prayer for Finding Joy and Laughter

Dear Lord,

Thank You for the gift of joy and the ability to laugh, even in the midst of life's challenges. I give myself permission to embrace moments of happiness without guilt, knowing that laughter and joy are blessings from You.

Help me to recognize the beauty in small moments and to allow myself to feel the lightness that laughter brings. Teach me that it is okay to experience joy as a part of my healing, and remind me that You delight in my happiness.

Thank You, Lord, for filling my heart with hope and for surrounding me with reasons to smile each day.

In Jesus' name, I pray,

Amen.

What moments of laughter or happiness have brought you healing today?

_____
_____
_____
_____
_____
_____
_____
_____
_____
_____
_____
_____
_____

Today I feel

I will feel better tomorrow when I…

_____
_____
_____
_____
_____
_____
_____

I am grateful for…

_____
_____
_____
_____
_____
_____
_____
_____
_____
_____
_____

Things to pray about…

_____
_____
_____
_____
_____
_____
_____

27

Each day brings new strength and healing.

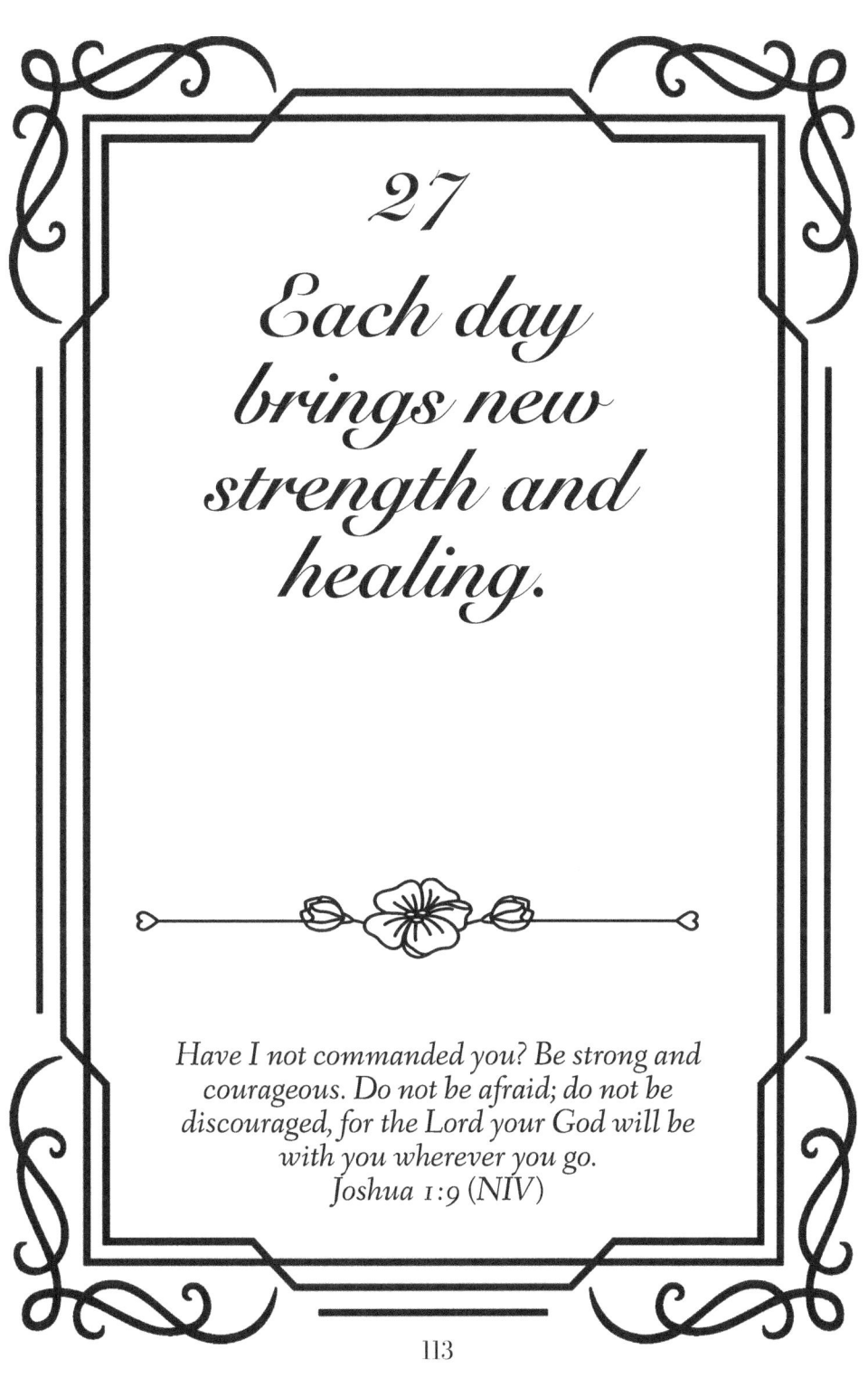

Have I not commanded you? Be strong and courageous. Do not be afraid; do not be discouraged, for the Lord your God will be with you wherever you go.
Joshua 1:9 (NIV)

Reflection

Even in the midst of pain, loss, and hardship, God's love remains unshaken. Written during a time of deep suffering, Lamentations 3:22-23 stands as a beacon of hope, assuring us that no matter how overwhelming life may feel, His mercy sustains us. It is His compassion that prevents us from being completely consumed by our struggles, offering us strength to endure.

God's compassion never fails. His tenderness and care meet us in our brokenness, providing comfort even when life feels uncertain. He sees our pain and is actively working to bring healing, restoring us with His grace.

Each day is a new beginning, a fresh outpouring of God's mercy. In seasons of grief, when sorrow feels endless, this truth invites us to take life one day at a time, trusting that God will provide the strength we need for each moment.

When grief shakes our faith, this verse reminds us that God's faithfulness is not dependent on our circumstances. He is steadfast, walking with us through every trial, offering hope and assurance that we are never alone.

Ultimately, this passage calls us to trust in His love, lean into His mercy, and embrace the promise of renewal. Even in our darkest seasons, we can hold onto the truth that His faithfulness is great, His compassion never fails, and His love will sustain us through every step of the journey.

A Prayer for Daily Strength and Healing

Dear Lord,

Thank You for the new strength and healing You bring with each day. Help me to trust that, even in small ways, I am being renewed and restored through Your grace. Teach me to embrace the present moment and to see each day as a step forward on my journey.

When I feel weak or discouraged, remind me of Your promise to sustain me and to bring beauty from my pain. Fill my heart with hope and gratitude for the healing that unfolds daily in Your perfect timing.

Thank You, Lord, for being my source of strength and for walking with me through this process of renewal.

In Jesus' name, I pray,

Amen.

What new strength or sense of renewal did you discover within yourself today?

_____
_____
_____
_____
_____
_____
_____
_____
_____
_____
_____
_____
_____
_____

Today I feel

I will feel better tomorrow when I...

_____
_____
_____
_____
_____
_____

I am grateful for...

_____
_____
_____
_____
_____
_____
_____
_____
_____
_____
_____

Things to pray about...

_____
_____
_____
_____
_____
_____
_____
_____

28

I am whole and complete.

And in Christ you have been brought to fullness. He
is the head over every power and authority.
Colossians 2:10 (NIV)

Reflection

Grief can leave us feeling empty, broken, and uncertain about how to move forward. Yet, even in our deepest sorrow, Colossians 2:10 assures us that we are still whole in Christ. The loss of a loved one may create a painful void, but our completeness is not found in circumstances—it is rooted in Him.

God's work in our lives is not undone by loss. While grief can make us feel shattered, Christ's presence fills the emptiness, offering strength, comfort, and healing. His authority extends over all things, including our pain, our future, and even death itself. Nothing is beyond His power to redeem.

In moments of sorrow, this verse reminds us that we do not grieve alone. Jesus walks with us, sustaining us through our pain and gently reminding us that life still holds meaning and purpose. His fullness reassures us that, though we mourn, we are not abandoned—we are held, loved, and made whole in Him.

Colossians 2:10 invites us to lean into Christ as our source of healing. In Him, we find the hope and courage to keep going, trusting that He is with us every step of the way, restoring and renewing us even through our grief.

A Prayer for Wholeness and Confidence

Dear Lord,

Thank You for reminding me that I am whole and complete through Your love and grace. Even in times of loss or uncertainty, I trust that You have created me with everything I need to live a fulfilling and meaningful life.

Help me to find confidence in my identity as Your beloved child, and teach me to embrace my independence with peace and gratitude. Let me feel the fullness of Your presence within me, knowing that I am never lacking when I walk with You.

Thank You, Lord, for making me whole on my own and for being the source of my strength and contentment.

In Jesus' name, I pray,

Amen.

In what ways do you feel whole and complete on your own?

_____

_____

_____

_____

_____

_____

_____

_____

_____

_____

_____

_____

_____

Today I feel

😊 🙄

😭 😢

I will feel better tomorrow when I...

_____

_____

_____

_____

_____

_____

I am grateful for...

_____
_____
_____
_____
_____
_____
_____
_____
_____
_____

Things to pray about...

_____
_____
_____
_____
_____
_____
_____

29

My experience has deepened my compassion.

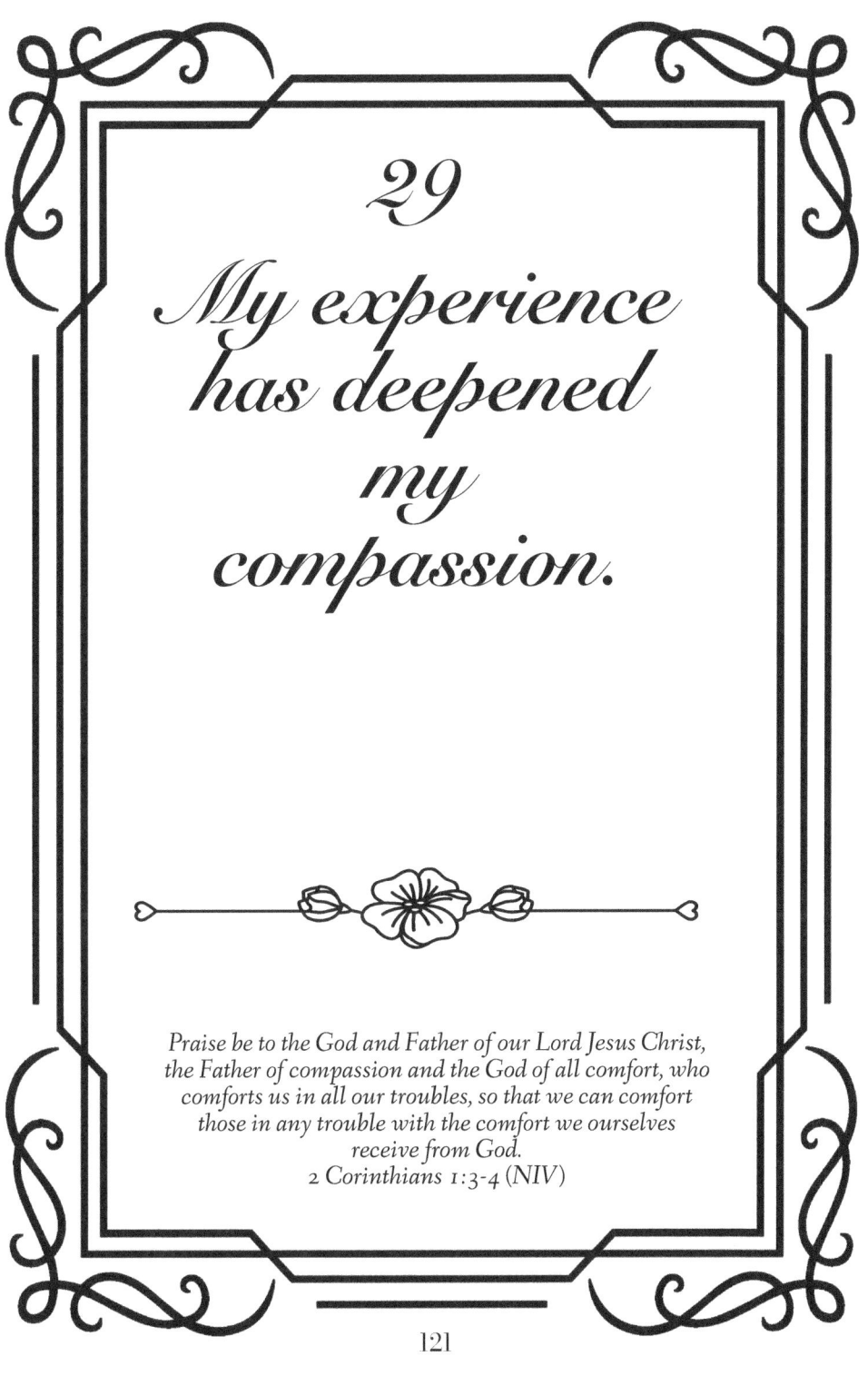

Praise be to the God and Father of our Lord Jesus Christ,
the Father of compassion and the God of all comfort, who
comforts us in all our troubles, so that we can comfort
those in any trouble with the comfort we ourselves
receive from God.
2 Corinthians 1:3-4 (NIV)

Reflection

God's compassion reaches us in our deepest pain, offering comfort that not only heals but also equips us to help others. He does not stand at a distance from our suffering—He meets us in it, bringing peace, strength, and hope that sustain us through every challenge.

2 Corinthians 1:3-4 reminds us that the comfort we receive from God is not just for ourselves; it is meant to be shared. When we experience His love in our grief, we gain a deeper ability to empathize with and support others facing similar struggles. Our pain, redeemed by His grace, becomes a source of healing beyond our own lives.

Grief and hardship can feel isolating, but this verse reframes our suffering as part of a greater purpose. God not only restores us but also transforms us into vessels of His love. When we extend to others the same compassion we have received, we become a living testimony of His faithfulness.

This passage is a call to trust that nothing we endure is wasted. Through His comfort, God weaves our pain into a story of redemption—one where we not only find healing but also become a source of hope for others who need it most.

A Prayer for Compassion and Growth

Dear Lord,

Thank You for using my experiences to deepen my compassion for others. Through my challenges and healing, You have opened my heart to understand and empathize with the struggles of those around me.

Help me to see others through Your eyes, offering kindness and support to those who need it. Let my compassion be a reflection of Your love and grace, and may it bring comfort and hope to those I encounter.

Thank You, Lord, for turning my pain into a source of growth and for teaching me to love more deeply through the lessons of my journey.

In Jesus' name, I pray,

Amen.

How has your experience helped you grow in compassion for yourself and others?

_____
_____
_____
_____
_____
_____
_____
_____
_____
_____
_____
_____
_____
_____

Today I feel

I will feel better tomorrow when I...

_____
_____
_____
_____
_____
_____
_____

I am grateful for…

_____
_____
_____
_____
_____
_____
_____
_____
_____
_____

Things to pray about…

_____
_____
_____
_____
_____
_____
_____
_____

30

I trust my ability to love again if I choose.

There is no fear in love. But perfect love drives out fear, because fear has to do with punishment. The one who fears is not made perfect in love.
1 John 4:18 (NIV)

Reflection

God's perfect love transforms us, replacing fear with freedom, peace, and confidence. Fear often arises from uncertainty, grief, or the unknown, but 1 John 4:18 assures us that God's love is complete and unconditional, leaving no space for fear to take hold.

In grief, fear can manifest in many ways—fear of moving forward, of forgetting a loved one, or of facing an uncertain future. Yet, God's love quiets these fears, reminding us that we are never alone. His love surrounds us, restores us, and assures us that even after loss, He is still guiding our lives with purpose and grace.

God's love is not conditional; it heals, redeems, and strengthens. When we trust in this love, fear loses its power. We can walk forward with courage, knowing that we are secure in Him, even as we navigate sorrow. His love also empowers us to continue loving others, even after deep loss, filling the spaces left behind and giving us the strength to embrace life again.

This verse invites us to rest in the assurance of God's perfect love. It calls us to live boldly, love deeply, and trust that His love is greater than any fear. Through Him, we are made whole—free to move forward, embrace new beginnings, and find hope even in life's hardest moments.

A Prayer for Trusting in Love Again

Dear Lord,

Thank You for creating my heart with the capacity to love deeply. Even after loss, I trust in Your ability to heal and restore my heart. If and when the time comes, help me to trust my ability to love again, knowing that love is a reflection of Your divine nature.

Guide me to approach new opportunities for love with wisdom and courage. Teach me to be open to the blessings of connection while honoring the love I have already experienced. May I trust in Your timing and Your plan for the relationships in my life.

Thank You, Lord, for being the ultimate source of love and for reminding me that my heart is capable of growth and renewal.

In Jesus' name, I pray,

Amen.

What gives you confidence in your ability to love again if and when you choose?

_____
_____
_____
_____
_____
_____
_____
_____
_____
_____
_____
_____
_____
_____

Today I feel

I will feel better tomorrow when I...

_____
_____
_____
_____
_____
_____

I am grateful for...

Things to pray about...

31

My life story is still unfolding.

For I know the plans I have for you, declares the
Lord, plans to prosper you and not to harm you,
plans to give you hope and a future.
Jeremiah 29:11 (NIV)

Reflection

Grief can feel like an endless season of uncertainty, where loss overshadows any sense of direction or hope. Yet, even in our sorrow, Jeremiah 29:11 reassures us that God's plans for our lives remain intact—filled with purpose, healing, and hope. Our pain is real, but it is not the end of the story.

When the future feels uncertain and unanswered questions linger, this verse calls us to trust in God's sovereignty. Though we may not see the full picture, He is lovingly guiding us through our pain toward renewal. His promise is not to shield us from suffering but to walk with us, using even our hardest moments to deepen our faith and resilience.

Grief can make the future seem distant or empty, but God's plans include restoration. The promise of "hope and a future" is a lifeline, reminding us that joy will return and that life still holds meaning. Each step forward, no matter how small, is part of His unfolding plan to transform our pain into something beautiful.

Jeremiah 29:11 is an invitation to lean into God's promises, trusting that He is not finished with our story. Grief, though heavy, is not permanent. With Him, healing, purpose, and joy are still ahead, waiting to unfold in His perfect time.

A Prayer for Trust in the Journey

Dear Lord,

Thank You for reminding me that my life story is still unfolding. Help me to trust in Your plan and to embrace each new chapter with faith and hope. Even when the path is uncertain, I know that You are guiding me toward a future filled with purpose and possibility.

Give me the courage to release fear of the unknown and to walk forward with confidence in Your goodness. Teach me to see every moment—both joyful and challenging—as a part of the beautiful story You are writing in my life.

Thank You, Lord, for being the author of my story and for walking with me every step of the way.

In Jesus' name, I pray,

Amen.

What aspects of your life story are still unfolding, and how do you feel about the journey ahead?

_____
_____
_____
_____
_____
_____
_____
_____
_____
_____
_____
_____
_____

Today I feel

I will feel better tomorrow when I...

_____
_____
_____
_____
_____
_____

I am grateful for…

_____
_____
_____
_____
_____
_____
_____
_____
_____
_____
_____

Things to pray about…

_____
_____
_____
_____
_____
_____
_____

www.ingramcontent.com/pod-product-compliance
Lightning Source LLC
Chambersburg PA
CBHW061651120626
46550CB00003B/906